How to Trace Your Ancestors Using a Computer for the Older Generation

Jim Gatenby

BERNARD BABANI (publishing) LTD
The Grampians
Shepherds Bush Road
London W6 7NF
England

www.babanibooks.com

Please Note

Although every care has been taken with the production of this book to ensure that all information is correct at the time of writing and that any projects, designs, modifications and/or programs, etc., contained herewith, operate in a correct and safe manner and also that any components specified are normally available in Great Britain, the Publishers and Author do not accept responsibility in any way for the failure (including fault in design) of any project, design, modification or program to work correctly or to cause damage to any equipment that it may be connected to or used in conjunction with, or in respect of any other damage or injury that may be so caused, nor do the Publishers accept responsibility in any way for the failure to obtain specified components.

Notice is also given that if equipment that is still under warranty is modified in any way or used or connected with home-built equipment then that warranty may be void.

British Library Cataloguing in Publication Data:

A catalogue record for this book is available from the British Library

ISBN 978-0-85934-720-4

Cover Design by Gregor Arthur

Printed and bound in Great Britain for Bernard Babani (publishing) Ltd

Preface

Many people move around the country and lose contact with their roots; some children grow up knowing little of their family history or the lives of their forebears. Fortunately the Internet has changed all that; nowadays anyone with a computer connected to the Internet can easily trace their family's journey through time.

This book starts off with an overview of the process of tracing your roots online, followed by a description of the hardware and software needed. The study of family history can benefit greatly when people pool their information electronically with others of the same name; this is covered in Chapter 3 together with the creation of a family tree using freely available online software.

Much information can be obtained about people and places using a search engine such as Google, described in Chapter 4; additional features such as Google Maps and Google Street View can provide accurate pictures of your family's places of origin which you may not be able to visit in person.

At the heart of online family history are the various genealogy Web sites. Chapter 5 gives an outline of the main features of some of the well-known sites. These enable you to search the official registers of births, marriages and deaths and the national censuses taken between 1841 and 1911. There are also specialist military and migration records and directories giving the location of early parish records and Bishops' Transcripts.

Later chapters describe searches of actual census records; also births, deaths and marriages and ships' passenger lists. The viewing of original records is also described, together with the ordering of copies of birth, death and marriage certificates.

The official records for Scotland are accessed separately by the ScotlandsPeople Web site and this is discussed in Chapter 7.

This book is by the same author as the best-selling and highly acclaimed "Computing for the Older Generation" (BP601).

About the Author

Jim Gatenby trained as a Chartered Mechanical Engineer and initially worked at Rolls-Royce Ltd using computers in the analysis of jet engine performance. He obtained a Master of Philosophy degree in Mathematical Education by research at Loughborough University of Technology and taught mathematics and computing in school for many years before becoming a full-time author. The author has written many books in the fields of educational computing and Microsoft Windows, including many of the titles in the highly successful Older Generation series from Bernard Babani (publishing) Ltd.

Trademarks

Microsoft, Windows, Windows XP, Windows Vista, Windows 7, Windows Live Mail, Office 2010, Word and Excel are either trademarks or registered trademarks of Microsoft Corporation.

All other brand and product names used in this book are recognized as trademarks or registered trademarks, of their respective companies.

Acknowledgements

I would like to thank my wife Jill and our son David for their help and support during the preparation of this book.

I would also like to thank the owners of the following Web sites who have allowed me to reproduce extracts from their sites:

Findmypast.co.uk, ScotlandsPeople, FreeBMD, The National Archives, Genuki, Ancestry.co.uk, The Genealogist, FamilySearch.org, Also Victoria Rowe, The Hollinsclough Web Site. Jackie Russell, the Dowler and Yates Family History. Mark Gatenby, the Gatenbys of Yorkshire. Philip Lindsay of xlab.co.uk, Newcastle on Tyne for the photographs from his Web site, shown on page 70. The Northumberland Collections Service for the images on page 71 from the Northumberland Communities Web site.

Contents

3

4

5

Entering Web Site Addresses

The study of family history using the Internet, relies heavily on the use of dedicated genealogy Web sites. Each of these sites has its own unique address on the Worldwide Web. Some of the most well known sites include findmypast.co.uk, Ancestry.co.uk, FreeBMD, and The National Archives. The reader may be confused because some sites are known only by their Web addresses (listed on page 8) while others use a shortened form, such as FreeBMD or Genuki.

To open a particular Web site, the address is typed into the address bar at the top of your Web browser. Most people use the Internet Explorer browser, as shown below.

The full Web address in this example (also known as a *URL* or *Uniform Resource Locator)* is actually :

http://www.findmypast.co.uk

However, in practice you can normally omit the **http://www** part of the address and simply enter into the address bar:

findmypast.co.uk

Please also note that some Web addresses use capital letters or a mixture of capitals and lower case in their names. For example, Ancestry.co.uk and FreeBMD. However, it's normal to use only lower case letters when typing in the address bar, such as:

freebmd.org.uk

Finally, always make sure you have the correct full *domain name* including the type of Web site and country. For example, entering **ancestry.co.uk** into the address bar opens a completely different Web site from **ancestry.com**. If you don't have the full address of a Web site, try entering what you know of the name into Google - this may produce a clickable link which will then open the Web site.

Conventions Used in this Book

Words which appear on the screen in menus, etc., are shown in the text in bold, for example, **Save As**.

Certain words appear on the screen using the American spelling, such as **Disk** rather than the British **Disc**, for example. Where the text refers directly to an item displayed on the screen, the American spelling is used.

Mouse Operation

Throughout this book, the following terms are used to describe the operation of the mouse:

Click

A single press of the left-hand mouse button.

Double-click

Two presses of the left-hand mouse button, in rapid succession.

Right-click

A single press of the right-hand mouse button. Right-clicking an object on the screen, such as a picture, normally displays a "context-sensitive" pop-up menu with options relevant to the selected object.

Drag and Drop

Keep the left-hand or right-hand button held down and move the mouse, before releasing the button to transfer a screen object to a new position.

Further Reading

If you enjoy reading this book and find it helpful, you may be interested in the companion book by the same author, **An Introduction to the Internet for the Older Generation (BP711)** from Bernard Babani (publishing) Ltd and available from all good bookshops. (ISBN 978-0-85934-711-2)

Genealogy Online

Introduction

Tracing your family history (or *genealogy* as it's more formally known), has never been more popular. The Internet has undoubtedly made the task much easier; thanks to Web sites such as findmypast.co.uk and Ancestry.co.uk, we now have instant access to millions of records, without ever leaving home. These records are based on the censuses from 1841 to 1911 and the Civil Registers of births, marriages and deaths from 1837 onwards. Another advantage of tracing your ancestors online is that you can get in touch with relatives anywhere in the world and rapidly pool your information. Old photographs such as the one below showing my wife's father, aunt and uncles around 1930 can convey a lot of information about earlier times. These pictures can be scanned and the images sent by e-mail anywhere in the world, arriving in seconds. This subject is discussed in more detail in Chapter 3.

You may find that some of your relatives have already created a family Web site. In my family, Mark Gatenby had already created a very comprehensive site with several family trees including my own. To this I was able to add my wife Jill and our sons David and Richard, circled in red on the right below. Also circled is my father's brother Harold Heslop Gatenby who emigrated to Canada. Through the ship's passenger lists in findmypast.co.uk I found the voyage which took Harold to Canada from Liverpool as a 22 year old, before starting his own prodigious Canadian family tree, which occupies the lower half of the family tree below.

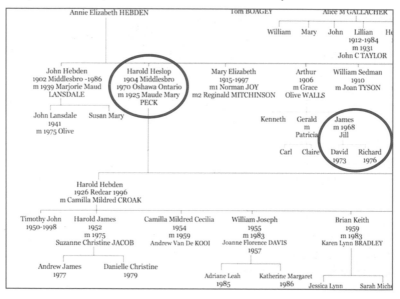

Through a dialogue which developed via e-mail and various message boards, I made contact with my cousin John Lansdale Gatenby, listed on the left above, who I had not seen for over 40 years. He had travelled extensively visiting relatives in New Zealand and Canada and shared with me his family knowledge and photographs. This included information about two uncles, Harold and Ronald, brothers of my father, who I had never met.

Why Trace Your Family History?

Many people have left their roots behind to live in distant cities and perhaps work in high pressure jobs in the modern world. They may find it reassuring to trace their family back to earlier times, when their relatives were part of a strong traditional community with a slower and simpler lifestyle.

My own purpose initially was to find out about grandparents who died before I was born; I was very surprised to discover that my maternal grandfather was born and bred in Scotland. My wife was curious to find about her forebears around the village of Flash in the Staffordshire Moorlands, the highest settlement in England, if not Britain, as sometimes claimed. As a result of our Internet searches we were able to visit my wife's ancestors' ruined homestead in a remote but beautiful area of the Peak District.

Some people may want to trace their roots to find out if they were connected to royalty or a famous adventurer, perhaps. You might equally find some unwelcome skeletons in the cupboard — perhaps a notorious criminal or murderer if you're very unlucky.

If you're related to someone famous (or infamous) for whatever reason, a search carried out after typing your name into Google, as shown below, is certain to yield a wealth of information.

Google	John Shakespeare	Search
	Search: ○ the web ◉ pages from the UK	

However, everyone should be able to find plenty of information about their own family because of the enormous volume of data available on the Internet from the Civil Registers, (births, deaths and marriages from 1837) and also national censuses, parish records and Web pages provided by various organisations.

What Can You Find Out About Your Family?

Searches using your home computer can yield some very interesting results. Here are some possible outcomes, based on our own research using the Internet:

- Finding out about relatives you never met, either alive or deceased, at home or overseas.
- Learning about ancestors' occupations, their homes, lifestyles and the area where they lived.
- Using census data to find out about family members and how they moved around the country. Obtaining copies of original census records.
- Knowing the address of a house, etc., finding out who lived there at the time of various censuses.
- Meeting up in person with long lost cousins and other relatives; communicating by e-mail, including free live video calls, anywhere in the world.
- Visiting the houses where ancestors once lived.
- Ordering copies of birth, marriage and death certificates and in some cases, wills.
- Joining online forums on the Internet where people can post requests for help in finding relatives and exchange information with others having the same surname.
- Constructing a family tree, using everyday office software and also using dedicated family tree software.
- Developing a sense of belonging to an area where your forebears lived, a spiritual home which may be far away from your present address.
- Helping children to understand their family background.
- Perhaps developing a more open-minded attitude if you find you have connections to people or places which were previously alien to you.

Sources of Information

After deciding which line of the family you wish to explore, you might adopt the following approaches to find information:

Traditional Methods

- Talk to other members of your family and consult any existing information already at hand, such as birth, marriage and death certificates. These will give dates and places of birth, details of parents and occupations.
- Visit churches and consult parish records, if available.
- Visit County Archives, Register Offices, etc., where parish and other records are kept on microfilm.

Using an Internet Search Engine

Enter your family surname or the name of an individual into a search engine such as Google; you may find some useful information straightaway. Search engines such as Google and Bing are discussed in detail later in this book.

Searching the Civil Registers on the Internet

Explore individual members of your family using a genealogy Web site such as findmypast.co.uk, Ancestry.co.uk and FreeBMD etc., (discussed shortly). These will allow you to trace Civil Registrations of births, deaths and marriages from 1837 onwards and enable you to order copies of certificates online (but delivered by the traditional letter post.)

Searching the National Censuses on the Internet

Some genealogy Web sites give access to the National Censuses, recorded every 10 years from 1841-1911. These list all occupants of a particular address at the time of the census, together with their age, date and place of birth and occupation. Copies of original census forms together with more legible transcripts can be viewed and printed. The initial searching is often free but you normally have to pay for transcripts and copies of original documents.

Genuki is a huge Web site compiled by hundreds of volunteers. It contains a multitude of links to Web sites and contact details for other organisations and individuals holding family information such as parish records and occupations for the UK and Northern Ireland, accessible by counties. In some cases CDs are available containing thousands of records.

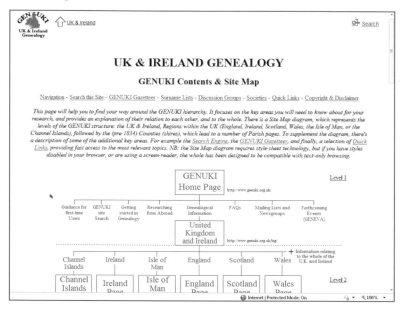

Online Forums

Some Web sites such as Ancestry.co.uk, host online forums or message boards where you can leave questions asking for information about relatives. These are then read and, if you're lucky, replied to by people with your own surname.

Re: Arthur, John , Redcar, Northallerton

Posted by: James Gatenby

Date: August 04, 2001 at 11:4

45   of 130

I am trying to find relatives of my father, Arthur Gatenby formerly of Redcar and Merchant Navy, later of Derby. Brother John was bank manager in Northallerton, retired to Thirsk. Also sister Mary who lived at Saltburn, married to Reg, I think. Other brothers included Bill an Ron, who may have emigrated to Canada.

Genealogy Web Sites

Try typing the word **genealogy** into an Internet search engine such as Google, as shown below. When you click the **Search** button a very long list of links to Web sites appears.

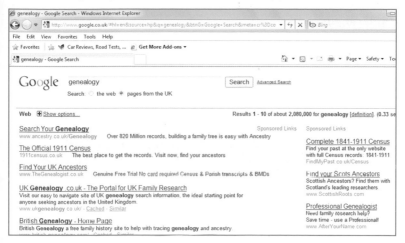

Click any of the blue, underlined links such as Search Your Genealogy below to have a look at the various Web sites.

Search Your **Genealogy**
www.ancestry.co.uk/Genealogy   Over 820 Million records

On the right-hand side of the list of search results shown above is a column headed **Sponsored Links**. These are companies or organisations who have paid to have their links included near the top of any search results involving genealogy Web sites.

Sponsored Links

Complete 1841-1911 Census
Find your past at the only website with full Census records: 1841-1911
FindMyPast.co.uk/Census

Find your Scots Ancestors
Scottish Ancestors? Find them with Scotland's leading researchers.
www.ScottishRoots.com

Examples of Popular Genealogy Web Sites:

Ancestry.co.uk

Claimed to be the largest collection of UK family records.

www.ancestry.co.uk

Findmypast.co.uk

Census records every 10 years from 1841 to 1911. Other records including births, deaths and marriages and there is also free software to create a family tree.

www.findmypast.co.uk

Genuki

This is a very large collection of genealogical records compiled by volunteers and covering various areas of the UK. Includes church, military and occupation records and also censuses.

www.genuki.org.uk

FreeBMD

Free Internet access to obtain copies of birth, death and marriage certificates for the period 1837-1983.

www.freebmd.org.uk

ScotlandsPeople

Over 80 million Scottish records covering Births, Marriages, Deaths and Census and Parish Records.

www.scotlandspeople.gov.uk

FAMILYSEARCH

A Web site set up by the Church of Jesus Christ of Latter-Day Saints. Provides free searching of millions of records and also free software for creating family trees.

www.familysearch.org

The National Archives

The Government's own archives containing millions of official records.   **www.national archives.gov.uk**

Essential Hardware and Software

The Computer

The work for this book is based on a PC computer running the Microsoft Windows 7 operating system. However, any computer manufactured in the last few years and any version of Windows will be more than adequate for this work. It's always a good idea to buy a machine with the fastest processor (CPU) and as much memory (RAM) as you can afford. A netbook or laptop computer will allow you to carry out your research from a your favourite armchair; using a desktop machine could banish you to a spare room or, in my case, a home office (i.e. shed), in the garden.

The Internet Connection

An Internet connection is essential for this work; Ideally you should have a fast *broadband* connection provided by a wireless router or access point. A router is very often provided free when you subscribe to an Internet Service Provider such as BT. The wireless router allows several computers to access a single Internet connection without the need to run cables around your home. If you are using an earlier *dial-up* Internet connection you can still do the necessary work to trace your family history but it will just take a little longer to find the information.

Further Help

More details on choosing and setting up a computer on the Internet are given in our companion book "Getting Started in Computing for the Older Generation — Windows 7 Edition" (BP 717) from Bernard Babani (publishing) Ltd, ISBN 978-0-85934-717-4, available from most bookshops.

The Printer

The printer is an essential part of any computer system and this is especially true for exploring your family history. You will probably want to build up your own word-processed notes and files of paper records, to be studied offline.

A great deal of material can be printed while you are online to the Internet. This includes copies of original census documents showing the occupants of certain households as shown below.

As shown above, these can be difficult to read and it's normally possible to print a more legible transcript in a modern typeface as shown in the extract below.

Address:	Cross Side, Quarnford						
County:	Staffordshire						
Name	Relation	Condition	Sex	Age	Birth Year	Occupation , Disability	Where Born
BRUNT, James	Head	Married	M	45	1836	Farmer Of 44 Acres Of Land	Quarnford Staffordshire
BRUNT, Margaret	Wife	Married	F	36	1845	Farmer Wife	Fawfieldhead Staffordshire
BRUNT, Sarah	Mother	Widow	F	78	1803	Annuitant Retd Farmer	Quarnford Staffordshire

It's usually possible to print any documents that appear on the screen. This includes the Civil Registers (lists of births, marriages and deaths, etc.) from 1837 and also the National Censuses from 1841-1911. Birth, marriage and deaths certificates don't normally appear on the screen — only reference numbers or indexes.

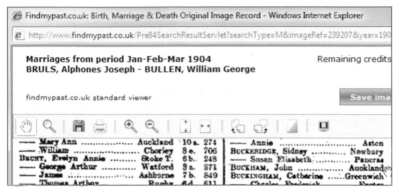

In the example above James Brunt's marriage certificate could be ordered using the dates above and the information below:

Brunt, Evelyn Annie	....	Stoke T.	6 b.	248
— George Arthur	....	Watford	9 a.	871
— James	....	Ashborne	7 b.	849

The indexes **7b 849** shown above enable you to order a copy of the marriage certificate online, to be sent in the normal post.

Extracts from parish records, etc., displayed on the screen as shown below, can be printed on paper for other people to view.

Quarnford Parish Register
These extracts relate to Hollinsclough residents only:

Baptisms, Burials & Marriages of Hollinsclough residents 1744 -60

First Name	Relationship	Surname	Abode	Date	Year
Mary	Daughter of William & Ann	Sellars	Gambolls Green	21st Dec	1744
James	Son of George & Martha	Wood	Cold-Shaw	9th Jan	1745

Jan 27th 1745 John Smith of Longnor & Mary Brunt of Cold-Shaw were married

Feb 21st 1745 William Goodwin of Quarnford & Sarah Moss of Gamballs were married

A good printer for this type of work is a *multi-function* inkjet or laser printer. An inkjet printer can be bought for under £50 and a set of four cartridges can be obtained for around £10 if you shop around on the Internet. A *wireless printer* will allow you to print documents on paper from a computer anywhere in your home — especially useful if you have mobility problems.

The Scanner

Apart from printing text and pictures from the computer screen onto paper, the multi-function printer also acts as a photocopier and a scanner. Separate "flatbed" scanners are also available starting at around £50. Scanning is useful for copying old photographic prints and storing the images on your hard disc. The print below shows my wife's family farm around 1930.

Once they are stored on your computer, photographs can be:

- Enhanced in a program like Adobe Photoshop Elements, to remove scratches or change contrast and brightness, etc.

- Sent to relatives as e-mail *attachments*.

- Posted to Web sites and "blogs" i.e. online diaries.

- Included in any family history documents you produce, such as family trees.

Essential Software

Microsoft Windows

Most computers are controlled by the Microsoft Windows operating system and this book has been prepared using the latest version, Windows 7. Most of the material in this book also applies to any version of Windows such as Windows XP and Vista. Any PC computer manufactured in the last few years will almost certainly have one of these versions of Windows installed.

Web Browsers

All versions of Windows include the Internet Explorer browser, a program for viewing and printing Web pages, launched by the icon shown on the right. Users of Windows 7, XP and Vista may choose to use an alternative browser, such as Mozilla Firefox, but the general methods described in the book will still apply.

Search Engines

This is a program in which keywords are entered, after which a list of links to Web pages containing the keywords is displayed. Google has been acknowledged as the leading search engine and it's freely available after entering the following into the Address Bar of a browser such as Internet Explorer.

The Google Web page opens with a search bar ready for you to enter the keywords which are part of your quest for family history.

Google UK

James Brunt Staffordshire Moorlands

Advanced Search
Language Tools

Google Search   I'm Feeling Lucky

Microsoft provides its own Internet search engine, known as Bing and shown below. You can open Bing by entering **www.bing.com** into the Address Bar of a Web browser such as Internet Explorer, as shown in the example on the previous page.

Arrows at the bottom right of the screen provide a choice of attractive backgrounds to Bing, such as the one shown above.

The Bing Search Bar above is displayed automatically if you make MSN your Home Page. The Home Page is the first Web page to be displayed at the start of an Internet session. The MSN Web site is opened by entering **http://uk.msn.com** into the Address Bar of a Web browser such as Internet Explorer. Then to make MSN your Home Page, select **Tools**, **Internet Options** and **Use current**, then click **Apply** and **OK**.

Most users will probably find either Google or Bing are perfectly capable tools to help with their research into family history, to complement the dedicated genealogy Web sites discussed later in this book, such as findmypast.co.uk and Ancestry.co.uk, etc. Search engines are discussed in more detail in Chapter 4.

E-mail Software

Electronic mail is an excellent medium for communicating with relatives wherever they are in the world. It's extremely fast and essentially free if you've already got a computer and an Internet connection. Apart from sending the electronic equivalent of a typed letter, you can also send copies of photographs and scanned documents. These are sent as *attachments* i.e. files "clipped" onto the main e-mail text message. I have used e-mail to exchange photographs and information with Canadian cousins I have never met.

Earlier versions of Microsoft Windows, such as Windows XP, had their own e-mail program called Outlook Express; the Windows Vista operating system included software known as Windows Mail. Windows 7 does not include an e-mail program (or *e-mail client*, as it's known). Instead, the latest Microsoft e-mail client, known as Windows Live Mail, can be downloaded free of charge after typing the following address into the Address Bar of a Web browser such as Internet Explorer.

Windows Live Mail is one of a suite of programs known as Windows Live Essentials, which can be downloaded from the Windows Live download Web site, as shown below.

Windows Live Messenger

Windows Live Messenger allows you to communicate instantly with people anywhere in the world. Your "chat " can include live text messages and a video link allowing you to see and hear the other person or people. To download this free software make sure **Messenger** is selected on the Windows Live Essentials download list shown on the previous page.

Windows Live Photo Gallery

This program can be used to edit, manage and share your family photographs. As mentioned earlier, you can scan old prints and store them on your hard disc. The Photo Gallery will allow you to improve the image and then it can be e-mailed directly to your relatives or posted to a photo-sharing Web site such as Flickr.

To download this free software make sure **Photo Gallery** is selected on the Windows Live Essentials download list shown on the previous page. You might also consider buying Adobe Photoshop Elements or PaintShopPro; these two photo-editing programs offer sophisticated tools allowing you, for example, to remove scratches and defects from images of old photographs.

Skype

This is a modern phenomenon which can be very helpful for anyone wanting to exchange family history information with relatives around the world. Internet telephone calls between two Skype-enabled computers or mobile phones are free world-wide.

The Skype software can be downloaded free after entering the following address into the Address Bar of a Web browser such as Internet Explorer. Then just follow the on screen instructions.

Skype 4.2 for Windows - Download the latest version of Skype

http://www.skype.com/

As shown below, you can make *video calls* with Skype with a computer equipped with a Web cam (plus speakers and a microphone). These accessories can be bought for a few pounds if necessary. Some laptops already have a built-in Web cam.

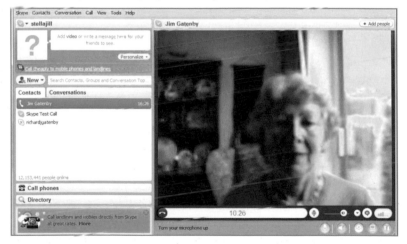

We use Skype to speak to and see our youngest son in his travels around the world as an airline pilot. Also by pointing a movable Web cam outside of a window, a relative can show you live pictures of the district in which they live.

Adobe Reader — the PDF File Format

You can usually "grab" the contents of a Web page on the screen and print them directly. However, this is not practicable for many larger documents, so they are made available in a form which allows them to be downloaded and saved on your hard disc. Then they can be viewed and printed whenever required. The format used for most of these documents is known as PDF or Portable Document Format. The advantage of the PDF format is that it can be read on any type of computer whether a PC or an Apple Mac or whatever. All you need is a copy of the Adobe Reader software, which can be downloaded free of charge from the Web address shown below.

> Adobe - United Kingdom - Windows Internet Explorer
>
> http://www.adobe.com/uk/

Simply click the button shown on the right to download a free copy of the Adobe Reader program.

As its name implies, you will only be able to read and save PDF documents using Adobe Reader; it cannot be used to create or edit documents. Originally you needed the Adobe Acrobat program to create documents in the PDF format. However, the latest versions of popular programs like Microsoft Word and Microsoft Publisher allow you to save documents as PDF files. This is very useful if you want to send a document to a relative, say, who doesn't use the same word processing software as you.

PDF is such a widely used format that books such as this one are saved in the PDF format. This is because printing firms in general can read PDF files and print from them, no matter what equipment they are using.

In the context of this book, many family history Web sites make documents available in the PDF format, ready to be downloaded from the Internet and saved on your computer.

A sample page from this chapter saved as a PDF file is shown below opened in Adobe Reader. The PDF format provides an extremely faithful reproduction of the original document, including any text and pictures. Separate pages are displayed and can be printed individually as required.

A PDF file is more compact than a file created in Microsoft Word for example. This makes it an ideal format for sending information over the Internet as an *attachment* to an e-mail (Attachments are discussed later in this book).

While researching your family history you will no doubt make up your own notes, booklets, etc. These might contain old scanned photographs, as discussed in Chapter 3, page 28. Also included might be images of any birth, marriage and death certificates and census returns. You would probably write up these notes in a word processor such as Microsoft Word; in Word 2007 and Word 2010, there is an option to save documents as PDF files. Then the document can be e-mailed to relatives, with whom you may be sharing family history information, anywhere in the world. If they have Adobe Reader they can read your documents no matter what type of computer system they are using.

Family Tree Software

When you've gathered all your information there are numerous ways to present your lineage in the form of a family tree. One approach is to use standard office software such as a word processor or a spreadsheet program like Microsoft Excel. Or you could buy a dedicated program like Family Tree Maker. Alternatively several of the well-known genealogy Web sites, such as findmypast.co.uk and Ancestry.co.uk provide free software allowing you to build your family tree online.

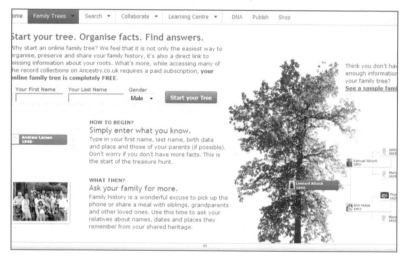

Lizard Tech DjVu

When you are looking at original handwritten census documents etc., on a Web site such as findmypast.co.uk, you can download a "plug-in" called DjVu. This is a program designed to improve the clarity of the scanned images of original documents.

Sharing Information

Introduction

Later chapters show you how to use your computer to search the national censuses and the birth, marriage and death indexes. Eventually you'll probably want to present your findings in a form that other people can easily read. You may want to create a folder of family trees, documents and photographs possibly to hand on to your children. By communicating online with relatives, both close and distant, you can benefit greatly from pooling your information. You'll probably find relatives online who've already done lots of research and are more than happy to share it with you. Some of the ways you can present and share your information are as follows:

- Create a family tree. This can be saved as a GEDCOM file (Genealogical Data Communication.) A copy of a GEDCOM can be given to someone else or uploaded to the Internet so that other people can view the tree.

- Old photographic prints can be scanned and the images added to a family tree.

- Scanned images of old photos, GEDCOM files and documents such as wills can be sent to relatives worldwide as e-mail *attachments*.

- Photographs can be uploaded onto easily accessible Web sites such as Flickr for other people to view.

- You can join a *message board* or *forum* for people with your surname. This will allow you to ask questions and exchange information with other people worldwide.

Creating a Family Tree

When you've gathered the information for your ancestors, the usual way to present it is in the form of a family tree. This could be created using a word processor or spreadsheet program. However, the easiest method is to use one of the online family tree programs, some of which are free. These can be found on the popular genealogy Web sites such as findmypast.co.uk or Ancestry.co.uk (shown below). These lay the family tree out online in a very professional manner and allow you to save it as a GEDCOM file on your hard disc. Then it can be sent by e-mail to other family members, wherever they are.

Shown below is part of the menu bar from Ancestry,co.uk. If you select **Family Trees** shown below, you can choose the option **Start a new tree**.

Click the box marked **+Add Yourself** as shown on the right.

A dialogue box appears as shown on the next page, ready for you to fill in the details of yourself or someone else in the family tree.

As you enter data for the family tree, as discussed on the next few pages, the work is being carried out online, i.e. on the Internet. The data you type in will be saved and the tree will still be there in future when you log on to the Internet. However, to create a copy of the tree on your local hard disc you must first *download* it from the Internet and then save it on your hard disc, as discussed shortly.

If you haven't got every piece of information such as **Birth Place**, for example, it doesn't matter — the family tree can still be created. A tree can be edited later to add any new information.

Add Yourself

Start with your own information; be sure to include a **first** or **last** name. For the most accurate results, enter dates in the format: 16 Aug 1925.

First and Middle Name

Jean

First and/or middle or middle initial

Last Name

Smith

Use maiden name, if applicable

Gender *(required)*

○ Male ● Female

Birth Date

1849

e.g., 18 Apr 1949 or About 1950

Birth Place

Canterbury

e.g., City, County, State, Country

Continue or Cancel

When you click the **Continue** button shown above, the tree appears with the new information added, **Jean Smith** in this example, as shown below. You can now continue adding family members by clicking on the various links such as **+Add Spouse**, **+Add Father** and **+Add Mother**, as shown below. Then continue for the grandparents and great grandparents, etc.

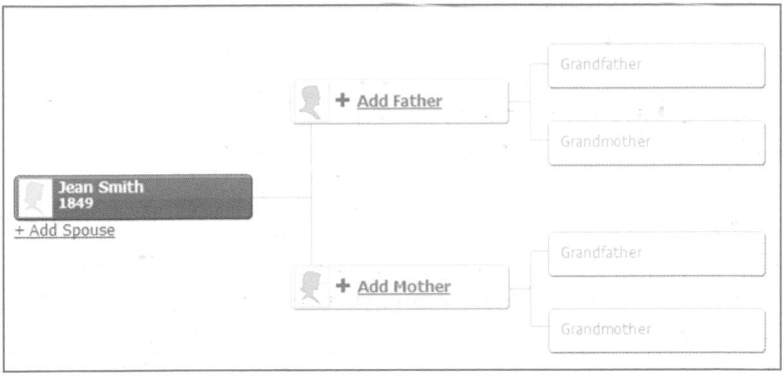

Grandfather

+ Add Father

Grandmother

Jean Smith
1849

+ Add Spouse

Grandfather

+ Add Mother

Grandmother

Shown below is a partially completed tree starting with my father, Arthur Gatenby.

Family Group Sheet			Print ▼
	John Gatenby 1852-1898	Jonathan Gatenby	▷
Arthur W Gatenby 1877-1934		Ann Wright	▷
	Mary Heslop 1856-1928	Thomas Heslop	▷
Arthur Gatenby 1906-1975		Jane	▷
	John Hebden 1850-1927	+ Add Father	
Annie E Hebden 1875-1947		+ Add Mother	
	Hannah 1851-1935	+ Add Father	
		+ Add Mother	

The leaves in the top right-hand corner of most of the entries indicate that Ancestry.co.uk has found additional information or hints, which may be of interest. Click the leaf icon to find out more about the hint. In order to read the information in the hint you may need to buy some credits from Ancestry.co.uk.

⊘ **Ancestry Hints for Annie Elizabeth Hebden** (learn more about Ancestry Hints)

Unreviewed Hints (4)	Ignored Hints (0)	Accepted Hints (0)

■ <u>Ancestry Family Trees</u>
We found hints with potential matches from 4 public Member Trees

Name: Annie Elizabeth Hebden
Birth: 1875 in Kildale, Yorkshire, [county], England
Death: 1947

🗎 <u>England & Wales, FreeBMD Birth Index, 1837-1915 Record</u>
Birth, Marriage & Death, including Parish

Name: Ann Elizabeth Hebden
Birth: Sep 1875 in Yorkshire - North Riding, United Kingdom

The hints are additional information which Ancestry.co.uk has found by searching the birth, marriage and death records and the national censuses. There is a button

enabling you to review the hint or ignore it if the information is not needed.

If you allow the cursor to hover over one of the names in the tree, a small window appears giving more information about the person, as shown below.

View profile allows you to add media to the person's entry on the family tree, such as a photo, story or audio or video clips.

You can correct any errors or add new information using the **Edit** option shown above. You are also informed of anyone else who is researching this person and are given the opportunity to communicate with them.

Saving a Family Tree as a GEDCOM File

While you are building up your family tree on the Internet, the data is saved on the Ancestry.co.uk server computer. Next time you log on to Ancestry.co.uk, the tree will still be there, even if you are using a computer in another part of the world. However, you may want to save a copy of the tree on your hard disc, or send a copy to someone else, perhaps for them to upload to a family Web site or to import into some genealogy software.

In creating a GEDCOM file, a family tree as shown on page 24, is converted into a text-only file; the GEDCOM format was developed by the Church of Jesus Christ of Latter Day Saints who are also responsible for the FAMILYSEARCH Web site. To create a GEDCOM in Ancestry.co.uk, select **Tree Settings** from the menu bar near the centre of the screen. Then from the lower right-hand side of the screen, click **Download your GEDCOM file**, as shown below

---

Manage your tree

Export your family tree data, as a GEDCOM file, to your computer.

[⬇ **Download your GEDCOM file**]

download tips

The **File Download** window should now appear on the screen. However, in some instances the coding for the GEDCOM file may suddenly appear on the screen as a text file, as shown in the small extract below.

```
1 GEDC
2 VERS 5.5
2 FORM LINEAGE-LINKED
0 @P781700300@ INDI
1 NAME Jim /Gatenby/
1 SEX M
```

In this case, click the **Back** button on your browser, and then right-click over **Download your GEDCOM file** as shown previously. From the menu which appears, select **Save Target As...**. The **Save As** window opens as shown below.

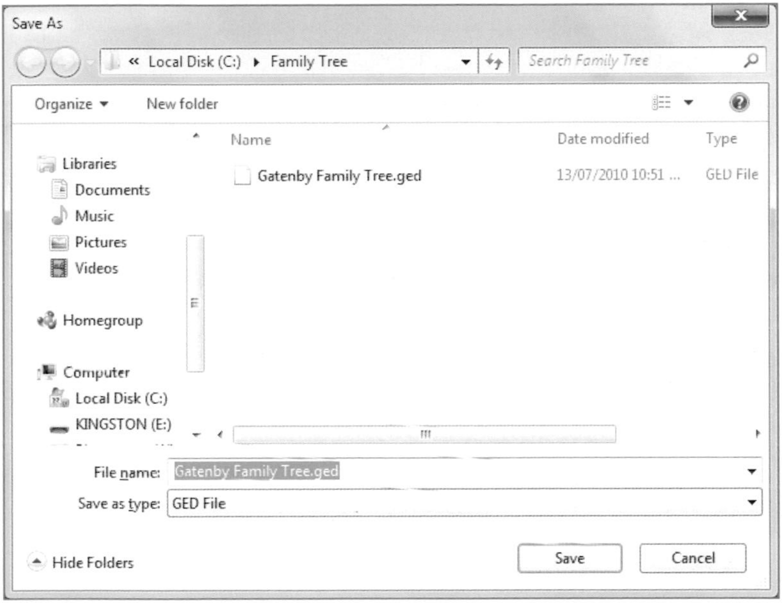

Select the location on your hard disc (usually the **C:** drive) where the GEDCOM file is to be saved. In this example, I have created a folder called **Family Tree** as shown at the top above. Then give your family tree a name as shown in the **File name** slot above. Finally make sure **GED File** is selected in the **Save as type** slot shown above. Click **Save** to place a copy of the file on your hard disc. To export the GEDCOM file to another location such as a removable flash drive, for example, make sure the new location is selected in the address bar. In the example below the GEDCOM file is being saved on a removable flash drive (also known as a memory stick) called **Kingston (E:)**.

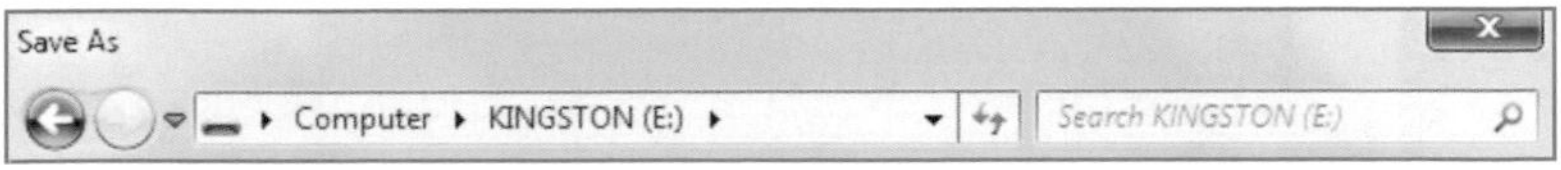

Scanning Photographs and Documents

During your collaboration with other family members, you are likely to want to exchange copies of old family photographs and documents such as birth, marriage and death certificates. An easy way to do this is to scan the photo or document and store it as a file on your hard disc. Then it can be e-mailed to your relatives, wherever they are. Flatbed A4 scanners can be obtained for under £50; you can also buy a *multi-function printer (MFP)* which includes an integral scanner for under £40. Place the photo or document face down on the bed of the scanner, close the lid and start the scanning software. In this example, the software SmartThru 4 is being used with a Samsung Colour Laser Multi-Function Printer.

As shown below, there are options to carry out a **Prescan**, followed by a **Scan** and then to send the scanned image to an **Application**, i.e. a program such as Microsoft Paint.

Saving a Scanned Image on Your Hard Disc

After clicking **Paint** and **Application** the image opens automatically in Paint, where it can be resized, cropped and rotated as required. The image can then be saved as a JPEG file, the universal standard for photographs. From the **File** and **Save As...** menu in Paint I have created a **New Folder** called **Scanned Images,** shown below. Alternatively the save location in the address bar could be a CD or removable flash drive, etc.

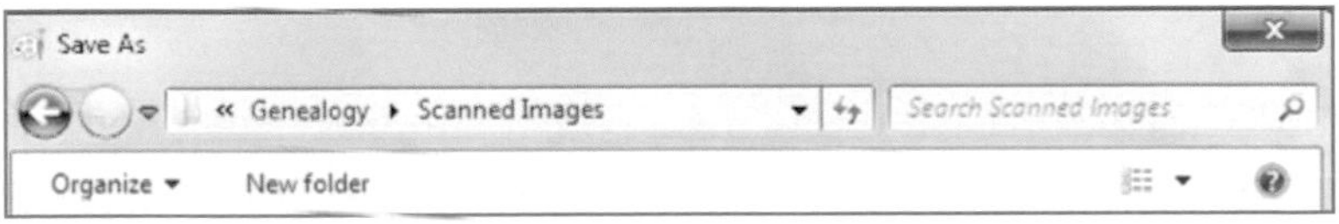

Then I have added my father-in-law's name, **Frank**, in the **File name** slot and selected **JPEG** in **Save as type**, as shown below.

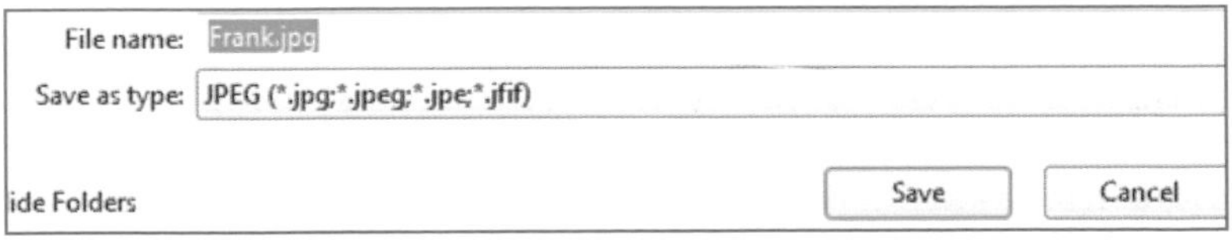

Clicking **Save** places a copy of the file in the selected folder.

After saving the photograph as a JPEG file, it can be displayed in the Windows Explorer as shown below. In this example, **Extra large icons** has been selected from the **View** menu.

Frank.jpg

In the example above, the scanned image **Frank.jpg** is saved in the folder **Scanned Images**, which I have created in a folder called **Genealogy** on my hard disc, labelled **Local Disk (C:)**.

Enhancing an Old Photograph

Once the image is saved as a file on the hard disc it can be sent anywhere in the world as an e-mail attachment, as discussed shortly. If the original photo was a bit tatty, the image could be opened in a program like Photoshop Elements or Microsoft Office Picture Manager. Then the image can be enhanced by altering the brightness and contrast, etc., and by removing scratches and other defects. Right-click over the image as shown above and then select **Open with** from the menu which pops up. Then select the program in which to open the image for enhancing.

| Open with | ▶ | ⊙ | Adobe Photoshop Elements 6.0 (Editor) |
| Restore previous versions | | ▦ | Microsoft Office Picture Manager |

Sending Scanned Images and GEDCOM Files

Apart from photographs, any sort of document can be scanned and the image saved as a file on the hard disc. This might include birth, marriage and death certificates, copies of wills or old letters between families, for example. Shown below in the Windows Explorer is an icon for a marriage certificate alongside of an icon for a photograph. Both represent JPEG files as discussed earlier. You could also include save a GEDCOM file in a similar folder, as discussed on page 26.

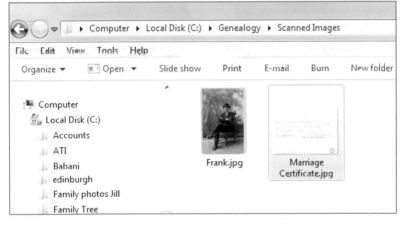

From this folder on the hard disc, copies of the files can be distributed to various destinations. Right-click over one of the icons such as the marriage certificate above, then select **Send to** from the menu which pops up. Now select the destination for the file, such as a **Mail recipient**, **DVD RW Drive (D:)** or the removable flash drive called **KINGSTON (E:)** as shown on the right.

If you copy a file onto a medium such as CD/DVD or flash drive, you could simply hand it or post it to your relatives; they could open a photographic image by double-clicking the icon in the Windows Explorer, as shown on the previous page. Or right-click the icon and choose **Open with** from the pop-up menu, then select a program such as Paint in which to view the image. A GEDCOM file needs to be uploaded to a Web site or to specialist genealogy software.

E-mailing Image Files as Attachments

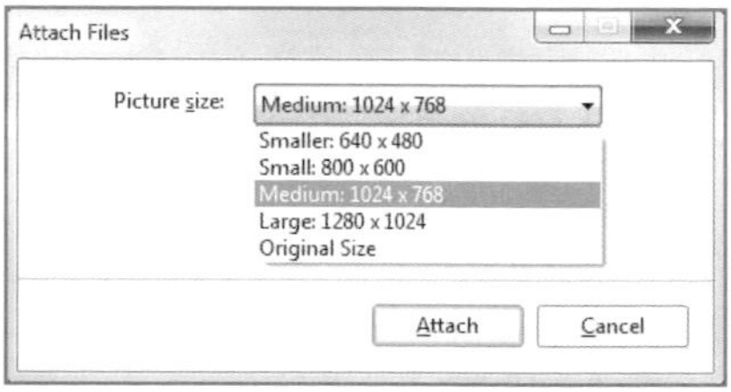

Right-click over the icon for the file, such as **Marriage Certificate.jpg**, in the Windows Explorer. Then select **Mail recipient** from the pop-up menu shown at the bottom of the previous

page. From the **Attach Files** window shown on above, you can reduce the size of the file if necessary, as this might be an issue with some e-mail systems. Now click **Attach** and your e-mail program opens up. Click **New** and a blank e-mail message opens with your image file, **Marriage Certificate.jpg**, already attached, as shown below.

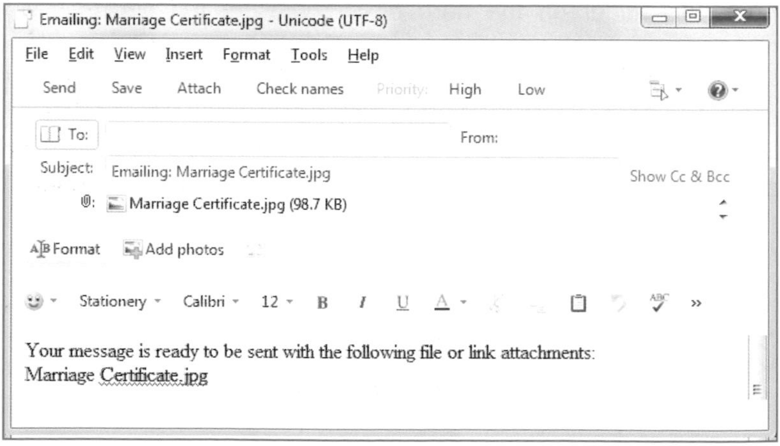

Now add the text of the e-mail and send it to your relatives, together with the attached image. When they receive the e-mail into their **Inbox** they can click the name of the attachment such as **Marriage Certificate.jpg**, for example, and select **Open** or **Save** from the menu which appears. In Hotmail the image is also displayed in the text area of the message, as shown below.

A saved image can be viewed later by double-clicking its icon in the Windows Explorer or by right-clicking the icon and selecting a program in which to view the image, **Open with**. Suitable programs to view an image include Paint and Microsoft Office Picture Manager. Then a copy of the photograph or document might be printed on paper and added to your family history folder.

A family tree saved as a GEDCOM file can also be e-mailed as an attachment in a similar way and then viewed after uploading to a genealogy Web site or special genealogy software.

Uploading Images to the Internet

Another way to share family photos and other images is to upload them to an image sharing Web site such as Flickr, at:

www.flickr.com

Message Boards

You can exchange information with people having the same surname as yourself by joining one of the message boards hosted by the genealogy Web sites such as Ancestry.co.uk and Genealogy.com. These are forums where you ask a question about your family and then wait for other family members to post replies. I posted a message on GenForum on Genealogy.com asking for details about family members, as shown below.

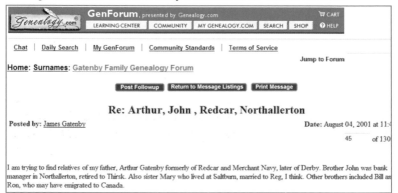

Several replies including the one from Mark below enabled me to find my own family tree, to correspond with a cousin in Canada and to renew contact with a cousin I had not seen for 40 years.

From these online exchanges I obtained a great deal of information and photographs about relatives in Canada and New Zealand who I did not even know existed.

Searching with Google

Introduction

Later chapters of this book show how major genealogy Web sites such as Ancestry.co.uk and findmypast.co.uk can be used to find family history information. These sites enable you to search through official records *online*, i.e. while connected to the Internet. The online records include the Civil Registers of Births Marriages and Deaths from 1837 and also the national censuses taken every ten years from 1841 to 1911. Worked examples showing searches of these official records are given later.

However, apart from the official registers, there is much useful family information stored on Web sites which individuals and voluntary organisations have created. These might include parish records or Web sites showing the history of a village, for example. A program called a *search engine* is designed to scan millions of Web pages and display a list of links to those Web sites which contain the *keywords* you are looking for. Google is the world's favourite search engine and can be launched for free after entering **www.google.co.uk** into the Address Bar of a Web browser such as Internet Explorer, as shown below.

Using Google to Search for a Person

You may find a lot of information about your relatives by searching with Google — or you may be unlucky and not find very much. This method depends on local organisations and individuals to make their information available on Web pages on the Internet. As an example, we might search for my wife Jill's grandfather, **James Brunt**, who we know was born in the remote village of **Flash** in the Staffordshire Moorlands. We could enter these details into Google as shown below.

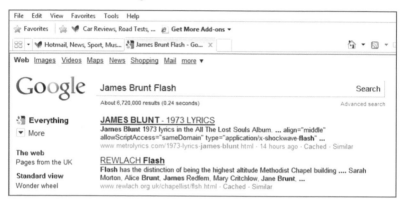

Surprisingly the first result involves the singer **James Blunt**. Obviously this result was not required in the context of our particular search and could have been eliminated by enclosing the name in inverted commas, as shown on the next page.

The effect of the inverted commas is to reduce the number of results from 6,720,000 to 396 as shown below and on the next page

Google "James Brunt" Flash

About 396 results (0.10 seconds)

When inverted commas are used Google only lists Web pages containing *exactly* what is within the speech marks. Without the speech marks you also get a lot of unwanted results where the keywords do appear on a Web page but they are separated, as in the case of John **BRUNT** and **James** ABBOTT shown below.

I3096: Fanny (ABT 1872 -   )
BIRTH: ABT 1788, Cocket Knowl,STS,ENG; CHRISTENING: 9 May 1788,
Flash,STS,ENG ... Family 1 : John **BRUNT**. MARRIAGE: 23 May 1891, Bedford Wesleyan
Methodist Ch,Leigh,LAN,ENG ... [840] PAR: **James** (1842-1904; s/o William, & Martha
ABBOTT; ...

Upper and Lower Case Letters

As shown in the results above and below, Google finds exactly the same number of Web sites regardless of the use of upper or lower case letters.

Google "james brunt" flash

About 396 results (0.08 seconds)

The first result in the list produced using inverted commas is a link to **REWLACH Flash**, a Web site about the history of Methodism in Flash, by North Staffordshire Methodist Heritage.

"james brunt" flash   Search

About 396 results (0.12 seconds)   Advanced search

REWLACH **Flash**
Flash has the distinction of being the highest altitude Methodist Chapel .... Abraham
Brocklehurst, Ann Brunt, Isaac Brunt, **James Brunt**, Mary Barber, ...

If you click the link **REWLACH Flash** shown above, the document opens as shown on the next page.

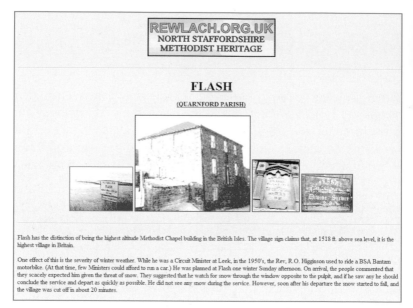

Cached Web Pages

The above document contains much interesting information about the village of Flash and the history of Methodism in the area. At 1518 ft above sea level it has been claimed to be the highest village in England, but perhaps not Britain.

Many online documents like this extend to several screens of dense text and it's not always easy to find the specific information you want. In this example we are looking for references to James Brunt.

The word Cached on a search result as shown below is a link to an earlier copy of a Web page. This may still contain all the information you need and this will certainly be true in a document like the above.

"james brunt" flash	Search
About 396 results (0.12 seconds)	Advanced search

REWLACH **Flash**
Flash has the distinction of being the highest altitude Methodist Chapel .... Abraham Brocklehurst, Ann Brunt, Isaac Brunt, **James Brunt**, Mary Barber, ...
www.rewlach.org.uk/chapellist/flsh.html - Cached - Similar

When you click on the word Cached, earlier versions of the Web pages are displayed and the keywords used in your search appear highlighted in yellow and blue, as shown below.

This is Google's cache of http://www.rewlach.org.uk/chapellist/flsh.html. It is a snapshot of the page page could have changed in the meantime. Learn more

These search terms are highlighted: james brunt flash

This makes references to **James Brunt** easy to find, as shown below in the North Staffordshire Methodist Heritage document.

me. That he was successful and his labours acceptable, appears evident from the fact that he was the Leader et one of his classes in his parlour on the Sabbath at the early hour of eight o'clock in the morning. Mr. bers being taken when a boy to this class, where he witnessed the faithfulness and tender earnestness of this fallen asleep

ies were :- 1st CLASS. Sarah Morton, Alice Brunt, James Redfern, Mary Critchlow, Jane Brunt, Martha Matthew Billinge, Zephaniah Brunt, Abraham Brocklehurst, Ann Brunt, Isaac Brunt, **James Brunt**, Mary Wood, Isaac Moss, Mary Barber, 4th CLASS. Betty Rigby, Mary Brunt, Isaac Billinge, Sarah Billinge, liam Needham, Elizabeth Bullock, Mary Wain, Sarah Slack, William Taylor, James Bestwick, Alice

The extracts from the REWLACH document state that Flash is in **QUARNFORD PARISH**, as shown near the top of the previous page. Changing the keywords in the Google Search Bar to include **quarnford**, as shown, below yields a different set of results. This time only 49 results, i.e. links to web pages, are found.

Google   "james brunt" quarnford   Se
                About 49 results (0.36 seconds)   Advance

Everything   Dowler and Yates Family History - Person Page 106
More   12 May 2010 ... James Brunt appeared on the census of 2 April 1871 at Summer Seat,
                Quarnford, Staffordshire. He was a farmer from 1881 to 1901. ...
                www.russellajj.co.uk/dowlerweb-o/p106.htm - Cached

As shown above, this result includes an extract from the **census** of **1871** and mentions that **James Brunt**, living at **Summer Seat**, was a **farmer**. However, Jill knew that her grandfather was not born until about 1879, so perhaps this James Brunt was Jill's Great Grandfather.

Clicking on the **Dowler and Yates Family History** link shown at the bottom of the previous page opens a Web site which includes members of Jill's family, the Brunts, including **James Brunt**, born **1836**, as shown below.

James Brunt
M, b. circa 1836, #3294

- James **Brunt** was born circa 1836 at **Summer Seat, Quarnford, Staffordshire.**
- He married **Margaret Beresford**, daughter of **James Beresford** and **Zilpah (?)**, circa Nov 1869 at **St Peter, Alstonefield, Staffordshire.**
- His marriage to Margaret **Beresford** was registered in the December quarter of 1869 in th **Ashbourne registration district.**
- James Brunt appeared on the census of 2 April 1871 at **Summer Seat, Quarnford, Staffor**
- He was a farmer from 1881 to 1901.
- He appeared on the census of 3 April 1881 at **Cross Side, Quarnford, Staffordshire.**
- He appeared on the census of 5 April 1891 at **New Cottage, Quarnford, Staffordshire.**
- He appeared on the census of 31 March 1901 at **New Cottage, Quarnford, Staffordshire.**

Further down the Web page is a link to another James Brunt born **1879**, son of **James** born in **1836**. Jill remembered that her grandfather had brothers including **Bower** and **George** and this confirmed that this **James Brunt born 1879,** was definitely her

Family: **Margaret Beresford** b. c May 1845

- ○ **George Brunt+** b. c 1870
- ○ **John William Brunt** b. c May 1872
- ○ **Mary Brunt+** b. c Nov 1874
- ○ **Sarah Ann Brunt+** b. c Feb 1877
- ○ **James Brunt** b. c Feb 1879
- ○ **Clara Brunt** b. 1881
- ○ **Joseph Brunt** b. c May 1883
- ○ **Bower Brunt** b. 1885

grandfather. Clicking on the link **James Brunt b. c. Feb 1879** shown above on the right provides more details, including the known fact that Jill's grandfather was a butcher in 1901.

James Brunt
M, b. circa February 1879, #3299

`Pop-up Pedigree`

- *Father*: **James Brunt** b. c 1836
- *Mother*: **Margaret Beresford** b. c May 1845

- *Relationship*: 2nd cousin 1 time removed of **Olive Yates**.

- James **Brunt** was born circa February 1879 at **Quarnford, Staffordshire.**
- His birth was registered in the March quarter of 1879 in the **Leek registration district.**
- He appeared on the census of 3 April 1881 at **Cross Side, Quarnford, Staffordshire.**
- He appeared on the census of 5 April 1891 at **New Cottage, Quarnford, Staffordshire.**
- He was a butcher in 1901.

All of this information was later confirmed by looking at the census data from 1841 to 1911. (Using the censuses is discussed in detail later.) However, thanks to the fact that the Dowler and Yates Family History containing the Brunt family, had already been put online, Google was able to provide a very quick and direct route to the information about Jill's grandfather. Google is also free, unlike some of the Genealogy Web sites.

The fact that you can get this information so easily is a huge advantage, especially if you live a long way from your family's roots. Or you may be disabled and unable to travel.

Fortunately we were able to travel to Flash in the Staffordshire Moorlands and see Jill's grandfather's grave. We were also able to discuss some of the places where her family lived. This included **Summer Seat**, mentioned on the previous page, where Jill's great grandfather was born in 1836 and where he was still living in 1871. We also learned that Summer Seat was built by the Brunt family on rented land, a practice apparently not uncommon in those days. The house was vacated in 1891 and has since been damaged by fire and fallen into disrepair. The following picture shows all that was left of Summer Seat in 2010.

Several Web pages refer to illegal activities around Flash. These include legends about the mysterious disappearance of peddlers who wandered the area looking for shelter. Wikipedia lists the making of counterfeit coins as another occupation and this is depicted in the sign for the New Inn at Flash, shown on the right. In the 19th century silk weaving and coal mining were major employers but these industries have now totally disappeared.

Parish Records

By entering the name **Brunt** and the name of the neighbouring village of **Hollinsclough** into Google, the resulting Hollinsclough Web site provides a wealth of information, including the following burial records. These show that there were Brunts living in the Flash and Hollinsclough area at least as early as 1607.

Henry		Hadfield	Pauperculi	Needle Eye	Dec 5th	"
Anne	Wife of Francis	Chapman	Husbandman	Holesclough	Jan 7th	1605
Ellen		Sellars	Begger	Duncoate Greave	Mar 1st	1606
Eliz	Wife of Roger	Naden		Holesclough	Nov 27th	1607
Thomas		Brunt		Burne Booth	Jun 24th	"
Eliz		Goodwin		Moscarr	Mar 19th	1608
Edw		Plante jun	Husbandman	Duncoategreave	Aug 13th	1609
Wm		Shiplebotham	Agricolae	"	Jan 15th	1610

Also shown in the above records are some early names of occupations such as **husbandman** (tenant farmer), **pauperculi** (poor person), **begger** and **agricolae** (farmer).

Using Google to Search for a House

Shown below is an extract from the birth certificate of Jill's mother Winnie, giving her father's name, James Brunt, her birth date in 1917 and the birth place as Stydd Hall, Yeaveley.

Stydd had been built as a manor house but in 1917 was being used as a working farm. By this time James Brunt had changed occupation from butcher to farmer. After carrying out a search for Stydd Hall using Google, numerous Web sites are listed giving a large amount of information about the history of Stydd Hall.

The Web sites state that Stydd is part Elizabethan and part Jacobean, with a large amount of medieval masonry. The hall was built on the site of a preceptory or headquarters of the Knights Hospitallers, a religious order founded in 1190. Extensive ruins and one wall of the original chapel remain, as shown below.

This picture was found on the Web by using Google Images.

Summary

This chapter has described the use of the Google search engine to find information about Jill's "Flash" grandfather, James Brunt. Some of the information obtained using Google was as follows:

- The names, birth places and occupations of Jill's great grandparents.

- Details of Jill's grandfather and his brothers and sisters, their births, marriages, homes and occupations.

- Details of the spectacular landscape and the lawless activities of some of the people, perhaps to compensate for the wild environment and difficult farming conditions.

- The strong presence of the Methodist Church in the area, including meetings at a Brunt family home.

- A large number of pictures showing the nature of the area, displayed after a search using Google Images.

- Early records from a neighbouring parish showing the Brunt family were present from as early as 1607.

- Details of the house where Jill's mother was born in 1917 and the site's history going back to 13th century.

The Brunt family searches with Google were very fruitful because Flash is a popular Peak District village and so there is a lot of information available on the Web. Also a lot of Brunt family records had been put on the Dowler and Yates family Web site by Jackie Russell. Some of this information is also available in the censuses, as discussed shortly, but you have to pay for it — Google searches are free. Similarly not everyone is born on the site of a 13th century Knights' preceptory described in numerous Web pages. Google is very useful for finding information about people and places, especially if you can't travel to an area. Some of this information may not be available in the official records accessed by the genealogy Web sites and discussed shortly.

Genealogy Web Sites

Introduction

The last chapter described the use of Google to search for information, after entering keywords identifying people or places. This method is only successful if other people have already "uploaded" relevant information onto accessible Web pages.

This chapter looks at some of the dedicated genealogy Web sites which have been set up to give online access to official records. These are mainly the Civil Registers of Births, Deaths and Marriages from 1837 and the National Censuses available every 10 years from 1841 to 1911. Most people alive at the time of a census should be listed, but there may be a few exceptions, e.g. if people were out of the country. Some parish records are also available online. There are also specialist registers giving access to military records and passenger lists of ships carrying emigrants to Canada, Australia and New Zealand, for example.

There may also be a genealogy Web site created by relatives of your own family. In my case, Mark Gatenby has created a very comprehensive Gatenby's of Yorkshire Web site, discussed later in this book. In my wife's family the Dowler and Yates Family History Web site provides much useful information.

Findmypast.co.uk   **www.findmypast.co.uk**

This site was previously called **1837online**. Activities available in findmypast.co.uk include the following:

- Searching the General Register Office databases for the indexes to births, marriages and deaths from 1837-2006. The indexes are used to place orders online for copies of the original certificates to be posted to you.

- Exploring the records of censuses taken every 10 years from 1841 to 1911, showing occupants of households, their ages, occupations and birthplaces.

- Examining parish records and specialist military and emigration records.

Charges

Initial searches are free but a charge is made when you view actual census returns or BMD indexes; payment is made by yearly or 6-monthly subscription or by pay as you go, e.g. £6.95 for 60 credits. An original census return costs 30 credits and a modern transcript costs 10. There is also a 14-day free trial.

Findmypast.co.uk includes a lot of help and advice about getting started in researching family history, including several online videos. Free software is provided enabling you to construct your family tree online.

GENUKI   **www.genuki.org.uk**

This is an enormous reference library on the Web. GENUKI is free to use and is run as a charitable trust maintained by volunteers. It directs a user to relevant Web sites where further information such as the addresses where parish records are kept or where a CD containing records may be obtained. GENUKI is organised in a hierarchical structure, allowing you first to select a country in the UK plus Ireland. Then you navigate down through the counties to find a parish or place you are interested in. For example, if you select Northumberland you are given a description of the county including the type of landscape, major towns and rivers and the main sources of employment.

Now click a link such as **Church Records** above and amongst an enormous number of further links are the following examples:

Emigration and Immigration

- Passenger list of the Guy Mannering which includes 58 persons from the Allendale area.

- Passenger list of the Lord Delaval which includes 50 persons from Berwick upon Tweed.

Click on a link to display a list of actual names of the passengers.

FreeBMD   **www.freebmd.org.uk**

This is a free Web site maintained by volunteers and sponsored by other Web sites such as Ancestry.co.uk. The aim is to simplify the task of finding the indexes or references which allow you to order a birth, marriage or death certificate. Previously you had to scan copies of the original sheets on the screen by eye until you found the person you wanted. The FreeBMD volunteers have transcribed millions of records from the original sheets so that they can now be searched by computer after entering a person's name. The results now appear instantly.

The following transcribed index was obtained by selecting marriage and entering surname and first name into FreeBMD.

This entry was created from the following transcription:					
Surname	**Given Name**	**District**	**Volume**	**Page**	**Transcriber**
Marriages Dec 1841					
GATENBY Jonathan		Whitby	24	607	rowenamd

The **Surname**, **Given Name**, **District**, **Volume** and **Page** above are enough to make an online order for the certificate from the General Register Office at www.gro.gov.uk. Clicking the link under **Transcriber** shown above displays the full name of the person who transcribed the indexes from the original sheets. Although freeBMD make no charge for searching for the indexes, you obviously have to pay a fee to the General Register Office (GRO) to cover the cost of producing and posting the certified copies of the birth, marriage and death certificates.

FreeBMD also allows you to view the scan of original document in various file formats, such as TIFF, JPEG or PDF, as discussed in Chapter 9. Then it can be saved on your hard disc and printed on paper.

Ancestry.co.uk   **www.ancestry.co.uk**

Ancestry.co.uk is the UK branch of Ancestry.com, a very large American Genealogy Web site. Billions of records are accessible from around the world. Ancestry.co.uk includes the following:

- U.K. Census records form 1841-1901.

- Birth, marriage and death records, from 1837-2005.

- Ships passenger lists.

- Military service records.

- Creation of an online family tree, including photographs.

As mentioned earlier, Ancestry.co.uk sponsors FreeBMD and gives access to their records. These have been transcribed into name searchable form by the FreeBMD volunteers. This means birth, marriage and death indexes can be found more quickly. In addition Ancestry.co.uk automatically inserts the indexes into an online order form, simplifying the process of ordering certificates.

Membership is by one of three levels of subscription, paid annually or monthly and there is a pay as you go option at £6.95.

Particulars of the person whose Birth Certificate is required	
Surname at Birth *	Gatenby
Forename(s) at Birth *	John
Reference Information from GRO Index	
Year (yyyy) *	1852
Quarter *	1
District Name *	Stockton
Volume Number *	10a
Page Number *	33

The Genealogist   www.thegenealogist.co.uk

This Web site offers a full range of genealogy services, including:

- Births, marriages and deaths from 1837 onwards.

- Census transcripts fro 1841-1901.

- Non-conformist, Wesleyan, Methodist, Baptists, etc., back to 1600.

- Parish records form 1538 onwards.

- Landowners with 1 acre or more in 1873.

- Wills and testaments.

- Knights of England back to 1127.

- Military records

Various subscriptions are available from £4.66 a month and there is a £5 pay as you go option. An associated Web site, www.genealogysupplies.com, sells genealogy software, books and CDs.

ScotlandsPeople   **www.scotlandspeople.gov.uk**

This provides a full set of records of the people of Scotland, including:

- Births, marriages and deaths from 1538-2006.

- Censuses every 10 years from 1841-1901.

- Wills and Testaments searches 1513-1901.

- Coats of Arms searches 1602-1907.

- Catholic Parish Registers 1703-1955

You can pay for searches at the rate of £6 for 30 credits; viewing a page of search results costs 1 credit and viewing an original image costs 5 credits. There is also a Getting Started guide to help you with your first steps in family history research.

Articles about Famous Scots from the past and present are also included and their are links to their biographical information and related documents.

No	Year	Surname	Forename	Sex	District	City/County/MR	GROS Data	Image	Extract
1	1888	WALLS	SARAH	F	BALLINGRY	/FIFE	408/00 0008	**VIEW (PAID)**	**ORDER**

Click here for printer-friendly grid

Page 1 (Free) ▼ of 1 (1 records)

Statutory Registers	Old Parish Registers	Census Records	Other Records
» **Births 1855-2006** » **Marriages 1855-2006** » **Deaths 1855-2006**	» **Births & Baptisms** 1538-1854 » **Banns & Marriages** 1538-1854 » **Deaths & Burials** 1538-1854	» **1841** » **1871** » **1901** » **1851** » **1881** » **1861** » **1891** » **1881 (LDS)**	» **Wills & Testaments Search 1513-1901 (Free)** » **Coats of Arms Search 1672-1907 (Free)** » **Catholic Parish Registers 1703-1955**

About ScotlandsPeople | Terms & Conditions | Copyright | Accessibility | Contact Us | Site Map | Search Site

ScotlandsPeople
Connecting Generations

The official government source of genealogical data for Scotland

FAMILYSEARCH   www.familysearch.org

This is a free Web site provided by the Church of Jesus Christ of Latter-Day Saints. It was started in 1999 and was one of the first genealogy Web sites. Founded in America, it provides access to worldwide databases including UK parish records.

Comprehensive help facilities are provided, including 5 online videos which can also be downloaded to your computer. There are separate videos for England and Ireland and some other countries.

The International Genealogical Index within FAMILYSEARCH is a major collection of parish records including England, Wales, Scotland and other parts of the world. It enables you to search for events such as births, deaths and marriages including those occurring before the start of the Civil Registration in 1837 in England and Wales.

RootsWeb   **www.rootsweb.ancestry.com**

This is one of the original genealogy Web sites and is now hosted by Ancestry.com. When I entered just the name Jonathan Gatenby into RootsWeb as shown below, it carried out a global search and produced some very impressive results.

Search RootsWeb.com			Search Ancestry.com		
Jonathan	Gatenby	Search			Search
First Name	**Last Name**	By Keyword	**First Name**	**Last Name**	Advanced

The results revealed a lot of information about my great, great grandfather including the names of his parents and brothers and sisters and his address in 1851. This search facility scans many worldwide databases; it may sometimes find records even if they occur before the start of General Registration in 1837.

RootsWeb enables family history researchers to communicate via a Message Board with other people interested in a particular surname. When I entered my surname into RootsWeb, 267 messages appeared, the second message involving my grandfather and great grandfather.

Arthur Wright Gatenby   Posted on: 14 Dec 1999, by
  Surnames > Gatenby

1881 census lists John Gatenby age 29 born 16 Thorn St Linthorpe,wife Mary age 25 born Riedale Yorks,Arthur W Gatenby son age 4 born Middlesbrough

Cyndi's List   **www.cyndislist.com**

This Web site is a gateway to a vast number of other genealogy Web sites. As shown below, there are over 270,000 links to help the family history researcher, covering an enormous range of topics such as guidance for beginners, worldwide censuses and numerous message boards.

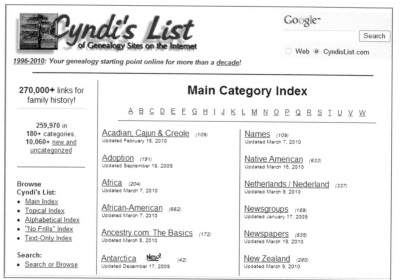

If you select **England** from the main index and then **History & Culture**, there are lots of interesting online articles, such as the History of the Census, shown in the extract below.

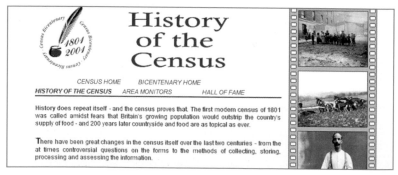

Using Census Records

Introduction

The census records from 1841 to 1911 enable you to find out where your ancestors lived and who the other members of the household were. My interest was to find out about my grandparents who died before I was born. All I knew about my maternal grandparents was that their surname was **Walls**. I used a copy of my mother's birth certificate as a starting point as it gives a person's full name, date and place of birth, their parents' names (including mother's maiden name) and father's occupation.

If you haven't got a particular birth, marriage or death certificate needed in your research, these can be obtained quite easily, as described in Chapter 8.

I decided to use the well-known genealogy Web site, findmypast.co.uk, which can be launched by entering **www.findmypast.co.uk** into your Web browser.

The examples in Chapters 6 and 8 of this book were carried out using findmypast.co.uk. All transcribed records are reproduced by permission of findmypast.co.uk. All original images are Crown Copyright, reproduced by courtesy of the National Archives, London.

Findmypast.co.uk

After entering the Web address as shown on the previous page, the findmypast.co.uk Home Page opens, as shown below.

In the top left-hand corner of the screen there is a **Welcome back** message, as I was a previous user of the site. This also states that I have 66 credits left. Otherwise you can look at the **Payment options** at the bottom left of the screen and either subscribe for 6 months or a year or choose **PayAsYouGo**.

Across the top of the screen is a menu bar with buttons for all of the main features of findmypast.co.uk, such as **Census** records, **Births**, **Marriages & Deaths** and **Migration**, **Military** and **Specialist Records**. The **Family Trees** feature on the menu bar above provides free online software with which to create and store your family tree. On the right of the screen there are links leading to help in getting started and various tutorial videos. In the lower centre of the screen are news items about the latest records to be added to findmypast.co.uk. In the centre of the screen is the **Search** feature discussed on the next page.

Starting the Search

Enter the first and last names of the person you are looking for, in this example my mother, **Olive Walls**. You don't need to enter the birth and/or death year unless you are searching for a name like **Smith** and are likely to get a lot of results.

Search Our Records

* Fields required

First Name

Olive

* Last Name

Walls

Birth Year   Death Year

Search ▶

Search Births, Marriages and Deaths   Search Census   Search Military

After I clicked **Search** the number of records found in the various archives was displayed, including 2 in the 1901 **Census** records.

1901 Census	2 records
1911 Census	6 records

The records in the 1901 Census can be dismissed since my mother was not born until 1904. However, the 1911 Census records should contain my mother's family and clicking on the highlighted text **6 records** above produced the following list.

Institution, Household or Vessel	Name	Birth Year	Age	Sex	Registration District	County	Household Transcript	Original census image
Institution	WALLS, Olive	1901	10	F	Birmingham	Warwickshire	VIEW	VIEW
Household	WALLS, Olive	1894	17	F	York	Yorkshire (East riding)	VIEW	VIEW
Household	WALLS, Olive	1907	4	F	Darlington	Durham	VIEW	VIEW
Household	WALLS, Olive	1904	7	F	Houghton Le Spring	Durham	VIEW	VIEW
Household	WALLS, Olive	1904	7	F	Rothbury	Northumberland	VIEW	VIEW
Household	WALLS, Olive May	1911	0	F	East Preston	Sussex	VIEW	VIEW

Viewing the Return for a Household

One of the records on the previous page agrees very closely with my mother's birth certificate, i.e. the correct name, **Olive Walls**, year of birth **1904** and place of birth **Northumberland**.

WALLS, Olive   1904   7   F   Rothbury   Northumberland

We can now choose to view a modern **Household Transcript** (costing 10 credits) or the **Original census image** (30 credits). The Household Transcript is shown on the next page.

Signing In or Signing Up

When you click either **Household Transcript** or **Original census image** and you are a new user, the window shown below appears. It will also appear if you are an existing user of findmypast.co.uk and have not signed in.

If you are already a user of findmypast.co.uk, you sign in with your username or e-mail address and password. If you are not yet registered, click **Sign up** to become a registered user of findmypast.co.uk. This will involve paying a subscription or making a PayAsYouGo payment, e.g. £6.95 for 60 credits. This is enough to view and print six census transcripts for a household or two original census images.

Sign in to findmypast.co.uk	Sign In	Not registered? Sign up
Once you're signed in you can:	Username or Email Address	
1. View millions of historical records.	Password	
2. Build your family tree for free using Family Tree Explorer.	Forgotten Password?	
3. Buy or renew a subscription or PayAsYouGo credits.	☐ Remember me ⓘ Do not tick this if you are using a shared computer	
	Sign In ▶	

After completing the signing in or registration procedure, the household transcript or original census image (whichever you selected earlier) will appear. A Household Transcript is shown on the next page.

1911 census - household transcription

Person: WALLS, Olive
Address: White House Ewesley Morpeth

Cost:
You will be charged 10 credits for a transcript and 30 credits for an image, unless you have
purchased a subscription for this set of records.

`REPORT TRANSCRIPTION CHANGE` `PRINTER FRIENDLY VERSION`

◄ census search results   all search results   redefine cu

Name	Relation	Condition/ Yrs married	Sex	Age	Birth Year	Occupation	Where Born
WALLS, Christopher	Head	Married 26 years	M	46	1865	Whinestone Hand-Breaker	Dumfries
WALLS, Mary Ann	Wife	Married 26 years	F	43	1868		Felling
WALLS, William	Son	Single	M	21	1890	Whinestone Hand-Breaker	Fife Shire
WALLS, Polly	Daughter	Single	F	17	1894		Embleton
WALLS, Christopher	Son		M	11	1900		Embleton
WALLS, Thomasina	Daughter		F	9	1902		Embleton
WALLS, Olive	Daughter		F	7	1904		Embleton
WALLS, Joseph	Son		M	5	1906		Embleton
WALLS, Catherine	Daughter		F	2	1909		Whitehouse
PATTISON, George Johnston	Boarder	Single	M	28	1883	Limestone Quarryman	Greennock
WHITE, Frank	Boarder	Single	M	36	1875	Whinestone Hand-Breaker	Edinburgh
JONES, Harry	Boarder	Single	M	24	1887	Whinstone Quarryman	Blarney U S A

Although the household transcription above is quite legible, you can click **PRINTER FRIENDLY VERSION** as shown above to produce the format shown in the small extract below.

1911 census transcription details for: **White House Ewesley Morpeth**

National Archive Reference:
RG14PN31188 RG78PN1785 RD569 SD1 ED14 SN52

Reg. District:	Rothbury	**Sub District:**	Rothbury
Parish:	Ritton White House	**Enum. District:**	14
Address:	White House Ewesley Morpeth		
County:	Northumberland		

Name	Relation	Condition/ Yrs married	Sex	Age	Birth Year	Occupation	Where Born
WALLS, Christopher	Head	Married 26 years	M	46	1865	Whinestone Hand-Breaker	Dumfries
WALLS, Mary Ann	Wife	Married 26 years	F	43	1868		Felling
WALLS, William	Son	Single	M	21	1890	Whinestone Hand-Breaker	Fife Shire

The results list displayed after a search include an option to **VIEW** the original transcript, as shown on the right below.

WALLS, Olive	1904	7	F	Houghton Le Spring	Durham	VIEW	VIEW
WALLS, Olive	1904	7	F	Rothbury	Northumberland	VIEW	VIEW
WALLS, Olive May	1911	0	F	East Preston	Sussex	VIEW	VIEW

The middle record above is my mother **Olive Walls** and **Rothbury** is the registration district for **Ewesley**, shown on the census return on the previous page. Searching the Internet revealed that Ewesley is a few scattered cottages and farmhouses with a quarry, disused railway line and a reservoir. Rothbury is a small market town a few miles away, situated on the river Coquet. According to various Web sites, Rothbury is in a beautiful area surrounded by hills such as Simonside and the Cheviot hills. Cragside nearby, was the first house in the world to have hydro-electricity and is now a National Trust property.

Now if you select **VIEW** under **Original census image** (the right-hand **VIEW** above) the original census image should appear if you are a signed in as a user and have enough credits. Otherwise you will be asked to sign in, register if a new user or credit your account with some money. Original census records cost 30 credits each. You can either use **PayAsYouGo** and **Buy Credits** as shown below or take out a subscription for 6 or12 months.

PayAsYouGo options

ⓘ How much do records cost to view?

	PayAsYouGo 280	PayAsYouGo 60
Valid for	365 Days	90 Days
Number of credits	280 credits	60 credits
	£24.95	£6.95
All Records	✓	✓
	Buy Credits ▶	Buy Credits ▶

Once your account has enough funds, the original transcription of the census records should appear as shown on the next page.

Viewing an Original Census Image

The census return filled in by the enumerator for the White House, Ewesley is shown below. To view different parts of the image, place the mouse cursor over the image and hold down the left mouse button. Now keeping the button held down, drag the image in the direction you require.

The menu bar across the centre of the screen has several useful tools, as shown below.

The hand icon on the left above permits scrolling of the image, by dragging, as described above. The single magnifying glass next to the hand above is used to enlarge a small area of the image at the current cursor position.

Next are two icons for saving and printing an image.
The two magnifying glass icons are used to zoom in
and zoom out of the image. The group of icons on
the right of the toolbar above are used to change the
width and height of the image, to rotate the image
through 90 degrees, to present white text on a blue background
and to display the image in full screen mode.

Enumerator's Information

One of the advantages of
viewing the original image is
that it contains more
information than the transcript.
This includes additional
information recorded by the
census enumerator. For
example, the census transcript

for my grandfather's household gave the address as White
House. Clicking **Description** on the right above produces the
information below. This shows that the full address was Ritton
White House and consisted of White House Farm and Cottages,
White House Lime and Whinestone Quarry, Cottages and Works.

Using the LizardTech Enhanced Viewer

Not surprisingly some of the scanned images of the old census returns are difficult to read, even after zooming in or using the magnifying glasses described earlier. On the right of the screen there is a link to download to your computer an enhanced viewer,

(As shown above there is also a button to allow you to save a copy of the image to your computer).

Click **Download free enhanced viewer**, as shown above then click the **Download** button next to your particular version of Windows, as shown below.

It is now just a case of clicking **Run** and **Next**, etc, and agreeing to allow the enhanced software to be installed on your computer. The enhanced viewer is called LizardTech DjVu and is a "plugin", a program used to improve another, larger program. This particular plugin is designed to improve the display of scanned images, such as the original census images, in the Internet Explorer Web browser.

When the installation is complete, click **Continue** and the original image will now be displayed in the LizardTech enhanced viewer, as shown on the next page.

You should see the LIZARDTECH logo near the top left of the screen and also the words  **findmypast.co.uk enhanced viewer**. The LIZARDTECH viewer has a different toolbar across the top of the screen, with more options than the standard viewer toolbar. Images should also load more quickly using the enhanced viewer.

© Crown Copyright Images reproduced by courtesy of The National Archives, London, England.

Recap of the Work So Far

So far we have used findmypast.co.uk to have a look at the census records for 1911, the latest available census. Starting with a person's name and place of birth you should be able to find them in any census taken in their lifetime from 1841 to 1911, unless they were away from home at the time of the census. Then you can see details of their address and other members of their household. As shown earlier, the census records can be displayed as a modern transcript in a perfectly legible typeface; alternatively you can view and print scanned images of the original documents. The original images can be difficult to read, although various magnifying tools are available. As just described you can also download a free enhanced image viewer called LizardTech DjVu. The original images contain additional enumerator information, not included in the transcripts.

Going Back in Time

The 1911 census showed my grandfather's family living at White House, Ewesley, near Rothbury in Northumberland. However, as shown below, several of the children, including my mother, Olive, were listed as being born before 1911 at Embleton.

Name	Relation	Condition/ Yrs married	Sex	Age	Birth Year	Occupation	Where Born
WALLS, Christopher	Head	Married 26 years	M	46	1865	Whinestone Hand-Breaker	Dumfries
WALLS, Mary Ann	Wife	Married 26 years	F	43	1868		Felling
WALLS, William	Son	Single	M	21	1890	Whinestone Hand-Breaker	Fife Shire
WALLS, Polly	Daughter	Single	F	17	1894		Embleton
WALLS, Christopher	Son		M	11	1900		Embleton
WALLS, Thomasina	Daughter		F	9	1902		Embleton
WALLS, Olive	Daughter		F	7	1904		Embleton
WALLS, Joseph	Son		M	5	1906		Embleton
WALLS, Catherine	Daughter		F	2	1909		Embleton
PATTISON, George Johnston	Boarder	Single	M	28	1883	Limestone Quarryman	Greenock
WHITE, Frank	Boarder	Single	M	36	1875	Whinestone Hand-Breaker	Edinburgh
JONES, Harry	Boarder	Single	M	24	1887	Whinstone Quarryman	Blarney U S A

The 1911 census above showed that five children were born at Embleton from 1894 to 1906. So the family should appear on the 1901 census. Using findmypast.co.uk and going straight to the **Census** section we can select **Search by person's name** and click the green **Search** button, as shown below.

Census	Search		PayAsYouGo Credits		Subscriptions
			Transcript	Images	
1911 census	Search by person's name	Search ▶	10	30	✓
	Search by address	Search ▶	10	30	✓
1901 census	Search by person's name	Search ▶	5	5	✓
	Search by address	Search ▶	5	5	✓

Note that transcripts and images for the 1901 census only cost 5 credits — cheaper than the 1911 census documents. At the time of writing the 1911 census records had not been released for very long.

This time I enter my grandfather's name, **Christopher Walls**, into the 1901 person search, as shown below.

No information other than the name was needed, as shown by the results below, which list two Christopher Walls in the registration district of Alnwick. Clicking to **View** the transcript for the first Christopher Walls at Alnwick revealed that they did live at Embleton as shown on the next page. The two Christophers were my grandfather and uncle, neither of whom I ever met.

Name ▾	Birth Year	Age	Sex	Registration District	County	Household Transcript	Origin censu imag
WALLS, Chris Jon	1898	3	M	Middlesbrough	Yorkshire (North riding)	VIEW	VIEW
WALLS, Christopher	1838	63	M	Caistor	Lincolnshire	VIEW	VIEW
WALLS, Christopher	1875	26	M	Prestwich	Lancashire	VIEW	VIEW
WALLS, Christopher	1854	47	M	Toxteth Park	Lancashire	VIEW	VIEW
WALLS, Christopher	1855	46	M	Wigan	Lancashire	VIEW	VIEW
WALLS, Christopher	1885	16	M	Wigan	Lancashire	VIEW	VIEW
WALLS, Christopher	1889	12	M	Howden	Yorkshire (East riding)	VIEW	VIEW
WALLS, Christopher	1866	35	M	Alnwick	Northumberland	VIEW	VIEW
WALLS, Christopher	1900	1	M	Alnwick	Northumberland	VIEW	VIEW
WALLS, Christopher A	1852	49	M	Prestwich	Lancashire	VIEW	VIEW

findmypast.co.uk

search with the experts ●

Friends Reunited   Now free, e

Welcome back Jim   credits left: 261   my a

| Home | Family Trees | Births, Marriages & Deaths | Census | Migration | Military | Living Relatives | Spec |

1901 census - household transcription

Person: WALLS, Christopher
Address: Blue Row, Embleton

Cost:
You will be charged 5 credits for a transcript and 5 credits for an image, unless you have purchased a subscription for this set of records.

REPORT TRANSCRIPTION CHANGE   PRINTER FRIENDLY VERSION

◄ census search results   1901 address search   redefine

Name	Relation	Condition	Sex	Age	Birth Year	Occupation Disability	Where Born
WALLS, Christopher	Head	Married	M	35	1866	Whinstone Breaker	Scotland
WALLS, Mary Ann	Wife	Married	F	33	1868		Blyth Northumberland
WALLS, Sarah Jane	Daughter	Single	F	13	1888		Scotland
WALLS, William	Son		M	11	1890		Scotland
WALLS, Mary Ann	Daughter		F	7	1894		Embleton Northumberland
WALLS, Agnes	Daughter		F	5	1896		Embleton Northumberland
WALLS, Christopher	Son		M	1	1900		Embleton Northumberland

The 1911 census shown on page 65 listed 5 children born at Embleton between 1894 and 1906. The 1901 census above shows my grandparents' address as Blue Row, Embleton. Also that two of the children were born in Scotland.

I now wanted to go back to see where my grandparent's and their children were living in1891. After clicking **Census** from the findmypast.co.uk menu bar shown above, select **Search by person's name** as shown below.

__1891 census__	Search by person's name	Search ►
	Search by address	Search ►
__1881 census__	Search by person's name	Search ►
	Search by address	Search ►

The 1891 census showed that at that time my grandparents were married and had three children, including Elizabeth aged 5; she didn't appear on the 1901 when she would have been 15. In 1891 the family were living at 12, Towns Street, Gateshead.

A similar search for my grandfather in the 1881 census showed a Christopher Walls living in Long Benton Village, Northumberland. The fact that he was born in 1865 in Scotland made it likely that he was my grandfather. If so, he had not yet married at this time and was living with my great grandparents, William and Elizabeth, born in Scotland and Ireland respectively.

1881 census - household transcription

Person: WALLS, Christopher
Address: Long Benton Village, Longbenton

Cost:
Transcriptions are free for this set of records. You will be charged 5 credits for an image, unless you have purchased a subscription for this set of records.

[REPORT TRANSCRIPTION CHANGE] [PRINTER FRIENDLY VERSION]

⇐ census search results   1881 address search   redefine current search

Name	Relation	Condition	Sex	Age	Birth Year	Occupation Disability	Where Born	Original census image
WALLS, William	Head	Married	M	37	1844	Highway Labr (Road Lab)	Scotland	VIEW
WALLS, Elizabeth	Wife	Married	F	42	1839		Ireland	VIEW
WALLS, Christopher	Son	Single	M	16	1865	Highway Labr (Rd Lab)	Scotland	VIEW
WALLS, James	Son	Single	M	11	1870	Scholar	Wallsend Northumberland	VIEW
WALLS, William	Son	Single	M	7	1874	Scholar	Wallsend Northumberland	VIEW
WALLS, Patrick	Son	Single	M	4	1877		Long Benton Northumberland	VIEW

From the fact that my grandfather appeared to have married between 1881 and 1891, I was able to use the findmypast.co.uk BMD records to obtain his marriage certificate as discussed shortly. I later acquired a copy of his birth certificate using the ScotlandsPeople Web site. These confirmed that his parents were indeed William and Elizabeth. A further search of the 1871 census showed my grandfather aged 6 living with his parents at Wallsend, Tynemouth. As my grandfather was born in 1865 in Scotland, 1871 was as far back as I could go in the censuses for England and Wales. However, more information on my grandfather was to be found using the ScotlandsPeople Web site as discussed in Chapter 7.

Using Google to Explore a Locality

If you live a long way from your family's roots, you can use a search engine like Google to find out a great deal about the area. As I live over 200 miles from Northumberland it was very helpful to find out about the area without leaving home. By entering **Ritton White House** (obtained from the 1901 census) into Google I quickly found a lot of links to very relevant Web sites.

These included an ordnance survey map which showed the exact location of the house where my mother's family lived in 1911. The Web site also stated that there had been a *bastle* at the site of Ritton White House. A bastle is a fortified farmhouse, commonly found along the border between England and Scotland. The bastle was designed to keep out marauding cattle rustlers known as *border reivers* during violent times in the area.

The 1901 census showed my grandfather's family living at Embleton, where my mother and most of the other children were born. Google searches revealed that Embleton is a small coastal village overlooking Embleton Bay as shown below.

© Philip Lindsay, xlab.co.uk, Newcastle on Tyne

These pictures were found by searches using Google Images. The ruined Dunstanburgh Castle lies on the coast at Embleton.

© Philip Lindsay, xlab.co.uk, Newcastle on Tyne

A whinstone (or whinestone) ridge separates the village of Embleton from the sea and there was a quarry shown below around 1880. The 1901 census, stated that my grandfather worked as a "whinstone breaker", presumably at the Embleton Quarries shown below.

It can be seen from the above photograph that apart from a great deal of man power, the quarry also used horses and steam locomotives.

Shown on the right is an extract from an Ordnance Survey map of Embleton in 1897. The Embleton Quarry appears near the top of the map.

The two images on this page appear on the Northumberland Communities Web site at:

http://communities.northumberland.gov.uk

They are reproduced here with permission from Northumberland Collections Service.

Summary

The census records can provide a wealth of information about your family from 1841 to 1911 as follows:

- Web sites like findmyast.co.uk make it very easy to locate a household at the time of a particular census.

- In some cases all you need is a person's first name and surname. You don't need to fill in every box. If a lot of people have the same name, you can narrow down the search using an approximate year or place of birth.

- A good starting point for family research is a birth certificate; if these are not readily to hand in the family they can be obtained easily from the General Register Office, as described in Chapter 8.

- The birth certificate gives the date and place of birth, the names of the parents including the mother's maiden name and the father's occupation.

- The information from the birth certificate will allow you to find who was alive at the time of a census. The census lists the names of everyone in the household, their occupations and dates and places of birth.

- Now you can work back through earlier censuses to trace your family members, perhaps living in different places and following different occupations.

- An Internet search engine such as Google can unearth a great deal of information about the history of a village or birthplace and display maps to identify the precise location of a house.

The findmypast.co.uk Web site, census records and my computer enabled me to find some of my roots in the wild and historic lands of Northumberland and also Scotland. Without online research I would not have known any of this.

Scottish Roots

Introduction

Chapter 6 showed how, using findmypast.co.uk and the census records, I discovered that my grandfather Christopher Walls was born in Dumfries in Scotland 1865 or 1866. (Birth years are not always completely accurate; for example, a birth at the end of a year might not be registered until the next year).

census search results		all search results					redefine cu
Name	Relation	Condition/ Yrs married	Sex	Age	Birth Year	Occupation	Where Born
WALLS, Christopher	Head	Married 26 years	M	46	1865	Whinstone Hand-Breaker	Dumfries
WALLS, Mary Ann	Wife	Married 26 years	F	43	1868		Felling

I also found out that Christopher later moved around Northumberland, first with his parents and then with his wife and children. For example, the 1901 Census recorded the family living at Embleton in Northumberland, as shown below.

census search results			1901 address search				redefine
Name	Relation	Condition	Sex	Age	Birth Year	Occupation Disability	Where Born
WALLS, Christopher	Head	Married	M	35	1866	Whinstone Breaker	Scotland
WALLS, Mary Ann	Wife	Married	F	33	1868		Blyth Northumberland
WALLS, Sarah Jane	Daughter	Single	F	13	1888		Scotland
WALLS, William	Son		M	11	1890		Scotland
WALLS, Mary Ann	Daughter		F	7	1894		Embleton

The 1901 Census also shows that two children, Sarah and William, my aunt and uncle, were born in Scotland in 1888 and 1890 respectively. To find out more about these Scottish connections I needed to use ScotlandsPeople, the official government Web site for genealogical data for Scotland. The Web site is opened by entering the following into the address bar of a Web browser such as Internet Explorer, as shown below.

http://scotlandspeople.gov.uk/

Getting Started

The ScotlandsPeople Web site opens at the Home Page, as shown below:

At the top right there is a button to allow new users to register and set up a username and password; existing users can simply select the login button and enter their username and password. The **Access Charges** link opens a page explaining the rate for viewing different types of document, such as birth, marriage and death records.

You can use the **Free Surname Search** window shown on the left above to find out which registers in ScotlandsPeople contain a particular surname. To view the actual records you need to have registered, purchased some credits (£6 for 30 credits) and signed in with your username and password.

Searching for a Birth in Scotland

I wanted to search for the birth of my grandfather, which I knew from the censuses was around 1865 to 1867. Under **Statutory Registers** shown on the previous page, select **Births 1855-2006**. Now enter the **Surname** and **Forename** and, if necessary, select the **Sex** (not essential in this particular case).

Search Statutory Register Births
Click here for more information.

Search		
Surname: *	Walls	?
	☐ Use Soundex	?
Forename:	Christopher	?
	☑ Return all forenames that begin with these characters	?
Sex:	Male ▾	?
Year Range:	1865 To 1867	?
	A birth that occurred at the end of a year may not have been registered until the beginning of the next year.	
County/City/Minor Records:	All Records ▾	?
District:	All Districts / ABBEY / ABBEY ST BATHANS	?

In the above example, I specified the birth year as 1865-1867. No district was selected. After clicking the **Search** button I was told that only 1 match had been found. To see the matching record, as shown below, click **Yes** and then **View**.

No	Year	Surname	Forename	Sex	District	City/County/MR	GROS Data	Image	Extract
1	1865	WALLS	CHRISTOPHER	M	TROQUEER	/KIRKCUDBRIGHT	882/00 0014	VIEW (PAID)	ORDER

At this stage I could not be certain that this Christopher Walls was my grandfather. The result above had the right name and year of birth but made no mention of Dumfries, which appeared as Christopher's birthplace on the 1901 census record. After a little research with Google and Google maps I soon realised that **Troqueer** mentioned above is close to the town of Dumfries and within the county of Dumfries and Galloway.

When entering the search criteria you don't always need to fill in every box. For example, when I missed off the year of birth and repeated the search, sixteen Christopher Walls were found. This time the only search criteria were the first name and second name and the fact that they were born in Scotland. However, only one was born in 1865 and all of the others were born in the 20th or 21st centuries. So this must surely be my grandfather.

No	Year	Surname	Forename	Sex	District	City/County/MR	GROS Data	Image	Extract
1	1865	WALLS	CHRISTOPHER	M	TROQUEER	/KIRKCUDBRIGHT	882/00 0014	VIEW (PAID)	ORDER
2	1904	WALLS	CHRISTOPHER	M	LOCHEE	DUNDEE CITY/ANGUS	282/05 0008	VIEW (5 CREDITS)	ORDER

Viewing an Image of a Birth in Scotland

Some birth records in Scotland have an image of the full birth details available to view on screen. This contrasts with the English records, where you must find the indexes of a birth and order a copy of the birth certificate to be posted to you.

In order to see the image (if available) click **View** as shown above. The fact that the record above says **PAID** is because I had already viewed the record on a previous occasion. Normally an image, as shown below, costs 5 credits to view the first time; you don't have to pay for repeat viewings.

As shown below, the image includes the usual birth certificate information; the date and place of birth, the name of the child, the names of the parents and the mother's maiden name. Also the address of the family and the occupation of the father.

An **ORDER** button on the right of the screen allows you to order (for £10) an official certificate containing the birth record.

The extract from the image at the bottom of the previous page was printed out and with the help of a magnifying glass I was able to see that Christopher Walls' parents were William and Elizabeth, the same names as the parents of Christopher Walls in the 1871 Census in Northumberland as shown below.

Name	Relation	Condition	Sex	Age	Birth Year	Occupation	Where Born
WALLS, William	Head		M	28	1843		Scotland
WALLS, Elizabeth	Wife		F	32	1839		Ireland
WALLS, Christopher			M	6	1865		Scotland
WALLS, James			M	1	1870		Northumberland

I was now confident that Christopher Walls born in Dumfries in 1865 to William and Elizabeth Walls was indeed my grandfather.

The birth image at the bottom of the previous page also showed that the family lived at 9, Church St, Maxwelltown, a part of the town of Dumfries. A quick search using Google Maps produced the map below, clearly showing Maxwelltown and Church St.

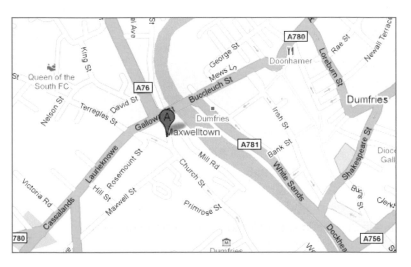

Finding Out About a Place

As I have never been to the area, I decided to use my online resources to find out about Maxwelltown, Dumfries.

Using Google Street View

Google have employed cars and other vehicles to film many areas of the world including the UK and the results are available through Google Maps. Type the name of the town or village into Google Maps and zoom in as far as possible. If the area has been filmed by Google a panoramic view at street level is displayed. You can scroll around the screen viewing the houses from different angles.

When I entered Maxwelltown into Google Maps, as shown below, I first located Church Street, as shown on the previous page. Zooming in produced the 3D Google Street View shown below.

Street View gives the actual house numbers and unfortunately it appeared that the house where my grandfather was born had been demolished to make way for a block of flats. However, Google Maps and Street View in particular are an extremely useful resource to get a feel for a district.

Searching with GENUKI

GENUKI is a tremendous source of information about people and places and can be launched from the address bar of your Web browser, as shown below.

When the GENUKI Home page is displayed, select **Contents & Search** and then click **Search**. Enter the name of the place, in this case **Maxwelltown** and click **Search Webpages**.

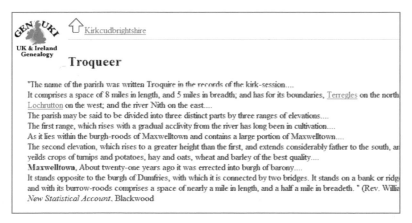

The search produces, amongst other things, an article describing the parish Troqueer in Kircudbrightshire which lies within Maxwelltown. These places were all mentioned on Christopher Walls birth record.

Searching with Google

A **Web** search with Google produced a Wikipedia page which informs that Maxwelltown was merged with Dumfries in 1929 and that Troqueer is a suburb of Maxwelltown. The market town of Dumfries lies on the east side of the River Nith with Maxwelltown on the other side.

A search for Maxwelltown in Google with the **Images** option selected produced a variety of thumbnail images as shown in the small sample below. Clicking on each of the thumbnail images leads to the full size image.

Web Images Videos Maps News Shopping Gmail more ▾

Google   Maxwelltown   Search

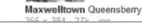

The Nith and **Maxwelltown** in
768 × 512 - 52k - jpg
chris.j.fergusson.20m.com
Find similar images

The Burgh of **Maxwelltown**
356 × 269 - 111k - jpg
futuremuseum.co.uk

The **Maxwelltown** rail
600 × 402 - 62k - jpg
railbrit.co.uk

Welcome the the
Maxwelltown

Maxwelltown Queensberry
356 × 384 - 27k - jpg

removed to **Maxwellto**
210 × 280 - 23k - jpg

Using only a computer and the Internet, I was able to find the exact address where my grandfather was born and get a good idea of the locality — without ever having visited the area.

Children Born in Scotland

I had found my grandfather on every census from 1871 to 1911, living in either Durham or Northumberland. However, two of his children, Sarah and William were born Scotland in 1888 and 1890 respectively, as shown below in the 1891 census transcript from findmypast.co.uk.

Name	Relation	Condition	Sex	Age	Birth Year	Occupation, Disability	Where Born
WALLS, Cristopher	Head	Married	M	25	1866	General Labourer	Scotland
WALLS, Mary A	Wife	Married	F	23	1868		Co Durham Felling
WALLS, Elizabeth A	Daughter	Single	F	5	1886		Willington Co Durham
WALLS, Sarah J	Daughter	Single	F	3	1888		Scotland
WALLS, William	Son	Single	M	1	1890		Scotland

A search for Sarah Walls birth was carried out in ScotlandsPeople in the way described on pages 75 and 76, using **Births 1855-2006** under **Statutory Registers**. When Sarah's year of birth was not specified 41 results were found. Including a birth year range of 1886-1890 in the search criteria brought the number of results down to 3. Only one was born in 1888 and viewing the image, shown below, confirmed that this was Sarah, born to parents Christopher and May Ann Walls (formerly McKeown).

No	Year	Surname	Forename	Sex	District	City/County/MR
1	1888	WALLS	SARAH	F	BALLINGRY	/FIFE

A similar search found the birth record of William Walls, my uncle, born 1890, in the same place, Lumphinnons in Fife. No detailed address was given. Using a Google Web search, Google Maps and GENUKI as previously described I was able to get some knowledge about the village of Lumphinnons where the births of Sarah and William were registered.

Summary

- Scottish births, deaths and marriages are held in separate archives from those for England and Wales. The official government Web site for accessing Scottish records is ScotlandsPeople.

- Using findmypast.co.uk, the censuses of England and Wales provided names, birth places and birth years for relatives born in Scotland. These enabled the birth records to be found in ScotlandsPeople.

- In some cases the birth records in ScotlandsPeople provide an onscreen image giving full details about the birth, including the name of the child, date and place of birth and parents' names. The English birth records only provide an index, allowing a paper copy of the birth certificate to be ordered online. ScotlandsPeople also includes an option to order a certificate.

- Google Maps was used to find the town and street where a family lived, in an unfamiliar part of Britain.

- Zooming in as far as possible launches Google Street View. This displays panoramic views of the street from various angles. (Some areas may not yet have been filmed for Street View).

- The GENUKI Web site is a valuable resource for finding out about parishes, towns and villages. This includes historical information about places which will probably have changed a great deal in the last two centuries.

Births, Marriages and Deaths

Introduction

In 1837 it became mandatory to record all of the vital events, such as births, marriages and deaths of people in England and Wales. Similar legislation followed in Scotland in 1855. These databases are called the Civil Registers and are maintained by a government department known as the General Register Office (GRO). The information in these records is used to produce legal documents for each citizen, such as birth, marriage and death certificates.

As discussed shortly, you can use your computer to obtain the BMD certificates for people alive from 1837 onwards. All you need is their name, approximate date of the event and the place where the event (birth, marriage or death) took place. Web sites like findmypast.co.uk allow you to find the indexes for a particular certificate. Then a copy can be ordered online from the General Register Office, as discussed shortly. The birth, marriage and death certificates contain a lot of family history material. For example, the marriage certificate below shows that my great, great grandfather, Jonathan Gatenby's was a mariner and married in 1841 at Whitby, Yorkshire to Ann Wright. Both were 25 and living in Sleights. Their fathers, William Gatenby and Joseph Wright were both farmers.

Starting the Search

Having found out quite a lot about my maternal grandparents and their migration around Northumberland I now wanted to find out what I could about my grandparents on my father's side. They had also died before I was born. I knew that my father was born before 1911 in the Middlesbrough area. I should therefore be able to find the family in the 1911 census. First I entered my father's name, Arthur Gatenby and Middlesbrough into the findmypast.co.uk 1911 person search, as shown below.

This produced the two results shown below. The top result looked promising as I knew my father was born about 1906.

Name ▾	Birth Year	Age	Sex	Registration District	County	Household Transcript
GATENBY, Arthur	1906	5	M	Guisborough	Yorkshire (North riding)	VIEW
GATENBY, Arthur Wright	1877	34	M	Guisborough	Yorkshire (North riding)	VIEW

Clicking on **View** under **Household Transcript** shown above produced the census return shown on the next page.

1911 census - household transcription

Person: GATENBY, Arthur
Address: 31 Yeoman St Redcar Yorkshire

Cost:
You will be charged 10 credits for a transcript and 30 credits for an image, unless you have
purchased a subscription for this set of records.

[REPORT TRANSCRIPTION CHANGE] [PRINTER FRIENDLY VERSION]

⬅ census search results   1911 address search   redefine current search

Name	Relation	Condition/ Yrs married	Sex	Age	Birth Year	Occupation	Where Born	Original census image
GATENBY, Arthur Wright	Head	Married 9 years	M	34	1877	Steel Works Clerk	Yorks Middlesbrough	VIEW
GATENBY, Annie Elizabeth	Wife	Married	F	35	1876		Yorks Middlesbrough	VIEW
GATENBY, John Hebden	Son		M	8	1903	School	Yorks Middlesbrough	VIEW
GATENDY, Harold Heslop	Son		M	6	1905	School	Yorks Middlesbrough	VIEW
GATENBY, Arthur	Son		M	5	1906	School	Yorks Middlesbrough	VIEW
GATENBY, William Sedman	Son		M	0 (11 MONTHS)	1911		Yorks Redcar	VIEW

I knew that this was definitely my father's family because I knew that he had brothers John, Harold and William. I also new that the family had lived at Redcar at some stage. I now knew the full names of my grandparents, their address in 1911, the years they were born and married. Also my grandfather's occupation as a Steel Works Clerk.

This information should be enough to obtain the birth and marriage certificates of my grandparents; then to go back in time to obtain the certificates of great grandparents, etc. (This would cover births, marriages and deaths as far back as 1837).

The 1991 census transcription above showed that they had been married for 9 years in 1911, putting their marriage year at about 1902. Dates like this may only be approximate.

We now select **Births, Marriages & Deaths** from the findmypast.co.uk menu bar. After selecting **Marriages** as the event type as shown on the next page, an estimated date range is selected as 1901-1903.

As you can see on the next page, you can specify the quarters of the year when you think an event such as a marriage might have occurred. By default you will get lists of results from every quarter starting with Jan-Feb-Mar and ending with Oct-Nov-Dec.

Search 1837 to 1983 - Birth, Marriage and Death indexes

enter search criteria   **search tips**

Select an event from the drop down list

Event type: *   Marriages ▾

Select the date range. This can be a maximum of ten consecutive years between 1837 and 1983.

Date range - from: *   Quarter: Jan-Feb-Mar ▾   Year: 1901

Date range - to: *   Quarter: Oct-Nov-Dec ▾   Year: 1903

Please enter at least 2 letters of the last name and optionally a first name

First name: ARTHUR   (optional)

Last name: *   GATENBY   (minimum 2 letters)

Now click search. Mandatory fields indicated by a *.

CLEAR   SEARCH

As shown above, **First name** is optional when entering the search criteria. A sample of the results of the above search is shown below. Each line of results such as GARRETT.........GEORGE shown below, represents a page of marriages. The marriage of anyone called GATENBY married in that quarter will be listed somewhere on that page.

Your search results

Your search returned 12 results.   PRINT

Event: Marriages   Date range: Jan-Feb-Mar 1901 to Oct-Nov-Dec 1903
Last name: **Gatenby**   First name: **Arthur**

redefine search

First name on page	Last name on page	Year	Quarter	
GARRETT, Minnie Grace	GEORGE, Miriam Beatrice	1901	Jan-Feb-Mar	VIEW
GARLICK, Ernest	GATES, Mabel	1901	Apr-May-Jun	VIEW
GARRATT, William Herbert	GAZE, William Albort	1901	Jul-Aug-Sep	VIEW
GARNETT, Charles Joseph	GAUNT, William	1901	Oct-Nov-Dec	VIEW
GARNER, Emily	GAYTHWAITE, Margaret	1902	Jan-Feb-Mar	VIEW
GARSTANG, Mary	GELDARD, Jane Ann	1902	Apr-May-Jun	VIEW
GARTSIDE, Ernest	GELDER, Annie	1902	Jul-Aug-Sep	VIEW

To display the first page of marriages for Jan-Feb-Mar click **VIEW** on the right-hand side of the results list shown at the bottom of the previous page. Now scan the results on the screen and try to find the marriage you are interested in. (Similarly for a birth or death). You may need to use the zoom buttons to make the text more readable, as discussed in the last chapter. It may also be necessary to scroll the image by dragging to view every record on the page. If you have downloaded the LIZARDTECH enhanced viewer (also discussed in Chapter 6) you can use the horizontal and vertical scroll bars on the bottom and right of the viewer, as shown below.

If you don't know the exact quarter when the event occurred click **Close Window** shown on the right above. Now click **VIEW** for the next page of results, GARLICK.......GATES for Apr-May-Jun as shown at the bottom of the previous page. Scan this second page of results by eye and keep repeating this process until you find the required event (birth, death or marriage).

I found the record of my grandparents' marriage in the Oct-Nov-Dec quarter in 1901. I knew it was correct because my grandfather was born in Middlesbrough and his correct full name appeared on the 1911 census as Arthur Wright Gatenby.

The important information here is the group of characters on the right-hand side, such as **9d. 1144** as shown below. 9d is the volume and 1144 is the page where the marriage certificate appears on the original Civil Records at the General Register Office (GRO).

```
—— Wiiium ..................... Camberwell  1 d. 1638
GATENBY, Arthur Wright ......Middlesbro'  9 d. 1144
—— Emmie ........................... Leeds  9 b.  920
—— Isabell..
```

We now have enough information to order a copy of the original marriage certificate, as discussed shortly.

Searching for Births and Deaths

The previous pages described the method of obtaining the indexes for a marriage certificate

The same general method is used for birth and death certificates. After selecting **Births, Marriages & Deaths** from the findmypast.co.uk menu bar, shown on page 86, select the appropriate **Search** button for births or deaths. You can also use the drop-down menu shown below in the search criteria window to make sure the required event type is selected.

Search 1837 to 1983 - Birth, Marriage and Death indexes

enter search criteria	search tips

1 Select an event from the drop down list

Event type: *   Births ▼
                      Births

2 Select the date range.   Marriages
    This can be a maximum of ten Deaths   ars between 1837 and 1983.

Date range - from: *   Quarter: Jan-Feb-Mar ▼   Year:

Once you've obtained the indexes such as **9d 1144** in the example above you can order the birth, marriage or death certificate, as discussed on the next few pages.

Ordering Birth, Marriage and Death Certificates

Using the method just described I used the deaths section in findmypast.co.uk to find the indexes for the death certificate for my grandfather.

Gately, William E.	40	Paddington	1 a	110
Gatenby, Arthur W.	42	Manchester N.	8 d	816
— Clara	57	Guisbro'	9 d	640

A similar search for my grandfather in the births produced the following result.

GATELEY, John Patrick.............	Middlesbro'	9 d.	587
GATENBY, Arthur Wright..........	Middlesbro'	9 d.	547
— George Robinson.	Thirsk	9 d.	406

On the right-hand side of the findmypast.co.uk screen, click the link **order BMD certificates**, as shown on the right. A screen appears providing a link to order BMD certificates online from the General Register Office (GRO).

useful links & resources

→ payment options
→ getting started
→ knowledge base
→ order BMD certificates

Order BMD Certificates

A certified copy of a birth, marriage, or death certificate can be ordered online from the General Register Office (GRO). This service is available both to UK and non-UK residents and covers births, marriages and deaths registered in England and Wales, as well as certain registrations overseas.

Details are also given for ordering certificates by post or e-mail. I have ordered certificates online many times and they have always arrived in the post within a few days.

General Register Office
PO Box 2
Southport
Merseyside
PR8 2JD
certificate.services@ips.gsi.gov.uk

After you select the link <u>General Register Office (GRO)</u> shown on the previous page, you are automatically connected to the Government's Directgov Web site at www.direct.gov.uk. This includes help in researching your family history, as shown on the left-hand panel below. On the right is the link needed to **Order a birth, marriage or death certificate**.

▸ **Researching family history**	▸ **Birth, marriage and death certificates**
▸ First steps in researching your family history	
▸ Researching family history using official records	▸ <u>Order a birth, marriage or death certificate</u>
▸ Using the General Register Office to research family history	▸ Order an adoption certificate
	▸ Order a civil partnership certificate
	▸ More on ordering certificates

After you click the link above, the next screen gives more information about the methods and costs of ordering certificates.

Ordering certificates online

You can order births (full certificate only), marriage or death certificates online from 1837 onwards providing you have the General Register Office index reference. If you do not have the reference, you can order certificates for events from 1900 if you know the exact date of the event.

You can find out more about using General Register Office index reference in the article below.

Extra copies of the same certificate can be issued at the same time for all applications. There is a fee of £9.25 for standard service and £23.40 for priority service.

▸ Using the General Register Office to research family history

▸ Order certificates online ⌱

Now click **Order certificates online** shown above and the General Register Office Web site opens at www.gro.gov.uk. The first time you use the service you need to select **Registration** and enter details such as your name and address, e-mail address and a password.

After selecting the type of certificate required and the year in which the event was registered, you then enter the indexes you found in your searches of the original records. On the next page I have entered the indexes for my grandfather's birth certificate.

Particulars of the person whose certificate is required

Year birth was registered	1876
Surname at birth *	Gatenby
Forename(s) *	Arthur

Reference information from GRO Index

Year	1876
Quarter*	Oct, Nov, Dec ▾
District name*	Middlesbro
Volume Number*	9d
Page Number*	547

Select the type of service — despatched next working day or fourth working day at a cost of £23.40 or £9.25 respectively. Then check the details and pay by credit or debit card. Depending on the sending option you choose, a certified copy of the certificate will soon be arriving through your letter box.

Information Obtained from Certificates

I have copied the 1841-1901 information below from the birth and marriage certificates of my ancestors in the Gatenby line. All of the certificates were obtained by searching the GRO records using findmypast.co.uk and then ordering online.

Great great grandparents

1816	Birth	Jonathan (birth year deduced from marriage certificate).

1841	Marriage	Jonathan, 25 mariner of Sleights, father William, farmer.

Ann Wright, 25, spinster of Sleights.
Father Joseph Wright, farmer. Married at Whitby.

Great grandparents

1852	Birth	John, mother Ann, formerly Wright.

Father Jonathan, a sailor, Lower East St, Middlesbro'.

1875	Marriage	John, 23, accountant of Lower East St, Middlesbro'. Father Jonathan (deceased), sea captain.

Mary Heslop, 21, spinster. Father Thomas Heslop, shoemaker, Hutton Rudby. Married at Stokesley.

Grandparents

1876	Birth	Arthur, mother Mary, formerly Heslop.

Father John, a clerk of 73, Monkland St, Middlesbro'.

1901	Marriage	Arthur, 25, accountant, 10, Borough Rd West, Middlesbro'. Father John (deceased) accountant.

Annie Elizabeth Hebden, spinster, of Middlesbro'.
Father John Hebden, mariner. Married at Middlesbro'.

The following information may be included on birth, marriage and death certificates:

Birth Certificate

- Name and sex of child
- Date and place of birth
- Name of father
- Occupation of father
- Name and maiden name of mother
- Signature, description, residence of informant.

Marriage Certificate

- Names of bride and groom
- Ages and conditions of bride and groom
- Date and place of marriage
- Occupations of bride and groom
- Residences of bride and groom
- Fathers' names and occupations.

Death Certificate

- Date and place of death
- Name and sex of deceased, maiden surname if female
- Address
- Date and place of birth
- Occupation
- Cause of death
- Name of spouse (if applicable)
- Name and qualification of informant.

Summary

- The birth, marriage or death certificates of your relatives provide the information to start searching the General Registers of births, marriages and deaths.

- The census records discussed in the Chapter 6 can also be used as a starting point to trace your family members. For example, if you know the name of a person and where they lived, you should find their household in one or more censuses from 1841 to 1911.

- To be sure it is the right household, you might recognise the names of other members of the family, such as brothers and sisters of your parents or grandparents. The census gives the names, dates and places of birth of everyone in the household.

- You can now use this data to search the births GRO images in a Web site like findmypast.co.uk. Scan these quarterly sheets by eye until you find the name and place of birth you require. This will give you an index for the birth certificate, which can now be ordered online.

- With the birth certificate, you now have the names of both parents, including mother's maiden name and occupation of the father. Successively go back in time searching the General Registers of births, deaths and marriages to 1837, the start of General Registration.

- Marriage and death certificates are obtained in the same way as birth certificates. Details of a bride's father given on the marriage certificate enable you to use the General Registers and censuses to explore the female branches of a family.

Online research gave me the names, occupations and the places where grandparents, great grandparents and great, great, grandparents lived and were born. I would not have found this information by traditional methods of research.

Obtaining a Death Certificate

Introduction

Chapter 6 showed how findmypast.co.uk and the Census records can be used to find out a lot of information about households, with "snapshots" taken every ten years from 1841 to 1911. From the censuses I was able to discover that my grandfather Christopher Walls was born in Dumfries in Scotland 1865 or 1866. (Both years were given on different censuses; birth years are not always exact because, for example, a birth late in one year may not be registered until the following year.) The 1911 census extract below also showed that my grandparents had been married 26 years, making the year of their marriage about 1885.

census search results			all search results				redefine cu
Name	Relation	Condition/ Yrs married	Sex	Age	Birth Year	Occupation	Where Born
WALLS, Christopher	Head	Married 26 years	M	46	1865	Whinestone Hand-Breaker	Dumfries
WALLS, Mary Ann	Wife	Married 26 years	F	43	1868		Felling

From the censuses you should be able to extract a person's name, year of birth and marriage (if applicable) and the place where they were born. Then you can enter those details into a Web site like findmypast.co.uk and obtain the General Register Office (GRO) indexes and order the birth or marriage certificates. If you know the approximate date of someone's death, you can order a death certificate in the same way.

As the censuses only record information about people living at a particular time, I had no idea of when my grandfather died. He was 46 years old in 1911, but may well have lived for another 30 or 40 years after that.

The General Register Office Indexes

The GRO indexes of births, deaths and marriages are presented on the screen as typed sheets, as shown in the example below.

WAL

282

DEATHS REGISTERED IN JULY, AUGUST AND SEPTEMBER, 1937.

Name	Age	District	Vol.	Page.		Name	Age	District	Vol.	Page.
Wallace, Harry C.	68	Uckfield	2 b	166		Walley, Martha	80	Crewe	8 a	326
— James	34	Nthmbld. Central	10 b	432		— Samuel	62	Crewe	8 a	335
— James B.	13	Edmonton	3 a	707		— Thomas	61	Stoke T.	6 b	114
— Janet A.	3	Romford	4 a	569		Wallhouser, Phillipa	84	Chelsea	1 a	313
— Jessie M.	60	Birkenhead	8 a	504		Wallhead, John G.	0	Leeds North	9 b	345
— John	14	Hartlepool	10 a	106		— Thomas	67	Ormskirk	8 b	656
— Joseph	51	Skipton	9 a	37		Wallin, Nellie	57	St.Asaph	11 b	199
— Joseph	82	Newport	11 a	157		Walling, Albert E.R.	59	King's L.	4 b	293
— Margaret L.	28	Liverpool S.	8 b	187		— Charles	63	Kendal	10 b	737
— Mary	52	Auckland	10 a	169		— William	72	Preston	8 c	438
— Mary A.	30	Birmingham	6 d	479		Wallington, Benjamin	75	Ploughley	3 a	1163
— Mary A.	64	Redruth	5 c	174		— Cecil H.	53	Brentford	3 a	194
— Mary B.	58	Whitby	9 d	429		— Mary	0	Medway	2 a	890
— Philip H.T.	30	Sunderland	10 a	567		— Robert	69	Richmond T.	9 d	613
— Robert W.	81	Teesdale	10 a	212		Wallis, Alexander	62	Huddersfield	9 a	382
— Samuel	63	Eastbourne	2 b	125		— Amy	72	Salford	8 d	327
— Walter	68	Hampstead	1 a	311		— Annie	76	Bromley	2 a	632
— Walter G.	65	Newbury	2 c	276		— Annie R.	0	Tonbridge	2 a	946
— William	77	Newport	11 a	149		— Beryl G.	84	Panorus	1 b	101
— William R.	60	Barnet	3 a	540		— Caroline	79	Hartlepool	10 a	94
— William R.	10	Birkenhead	8 a	484		— Catherine	86	Leeds North	9 b	370
— William R.	63	Birkenhead	8 a	509		— Charles	78	Tadcaster	9 a	754
Wallage, George	80	Erpingham	4 b	64		— Eliza	74	Stroud	2 a	852
— Rebecca	64	Cambridge	3 b	406		— Elizabeth	78	Henley	3 a	1147
Wallam, Rhoda	54	Barnsley	9 c	165		— Ellen	57	Bedford	3 b	303
Wallbank, Clara	63	Islington	1 a	226		— Ellen M.	58	Lichfield	6 b	561
— Elizabeth A.	72	Lichfield	6 b	377		— Emily M.	65	Southampton	2 c	48
— Louisa E.	85	Birmingham	6 d	456		— Frank	3	St.Albans	3 a	907
— Sarah	89	Ormskirk	8 b	655		— Frederick	6	Walsall	6 b	370
Wallbridge, George H.	19	I.Wight	2 b	750		— Frederick C.	0	Kensington	1 a	149

Each sheet above represents the deaths for one quarter of a year, for names within a certain alphabetic range. The sheet above covers July, August and September 1937, for names beginning with the letters WAL. To find a death index over say a 30 or 40 year period you might have to scan by eye well over 100 similar sheets until you found the one you want. Each sheet viewed would have to paid for and then the most likely death certificates would have to be ordered.

The problem is that the death records for each person above are not separate entities which can be searched by computer. They are all just part of a single scanned image, like a photograph.

The Web sites FreeBMD and Ancestry.co.uk provide *transcribed* GRO indexes which are searchable by computer, as discussed on the following pages. Transcribing the indexes by the volunteers of FreeBMD is an ongoing process, so some pages of records may not yet be available for computerised searching. At the time of writing approximately 200 million records have been transcribed.

FreeBMD

FreeBMD is a charitable Web site created by thousands of volunteers whose aim is to make the indexes searchable, free of charge. So instead of scanning the original record sheets on the screen by eye until you find the one you want, the FreeBMD search facility will quickly find the indexes for you. This is because the volunteers have undertaken the massive task of transcribing the indexes into a form readable by computer.

You can open the FreeBMD Web site by entering the address into a Web browser such as Internet Explorer.

> FreeBMD Home Page - Windows Internet Explorer
>
> http://www.freebmd.org.uk/

(To save time you can usually miss out the **http://www.** part of the Web site address, also known as a URL or "Uniform Resource Locator".)

The FreeBMD Web site opens at the Home Page, as shown below. There are links to associated Web sites such as FreeCEN, FreeREG (parish registers) and also to Ancestry.co.uk and findmypast.co.uk..

FreeBMD is sponsored by the RootsWeb, Ancestry.co.uk and The Bunker Web sites.

Searching With FreeBMD

Enter the surname and first name(s) of the person as shown below. You must also select one of the types of search, births, marriages or deaths; selecting **All Types** will produce indexes for all of the available records for a person.

			Districts	
Type	All Types Births Deaths Marriages			All Districts Aberayron (to Jun1936) Aberconwy (from Sep1975) Abergavenny (to 1958) Aberystwyth (to Jun1936) Abingdon Acle (1939-Mar1974) Alcester Alderbury (to Jun1895) Aldershot (Dec1932-Mar1974) Aldridge & Brownhills (Jun1966-Mar1974) Aled (Dec1935-Mar1974) Alnwick (to 1936) Alresford (to Sep1932)
Surname	Walls			
First name(s)	Christopher			
Spouse/Mother surname				
Spouse first name(s)				
Death age/DoB				
Date range	Mar ▾	to Dec ▾		
Volume/Page	/		Counties	
Options	☐ Mono ☐ Exact match on first names ☐ Phonetic search surnames ☐ Match only recorded ages			All Counties Anglesey (to Mar1974) Avon (from Jun1974) Bedfordshire Berkshire Breconshire (to Mar1974)

| Find | Count | Reset | | Saved | Filename: |

When you click **Find**, a list of the available indexes is displayed. In my grandfather's case only his marriage in Tynemouth in 1885 was listed as shown below. His birth was not listed because it was in Scotland, as previously discussed.

Marriages Sep 1885 (>99%)

| **Walls** | **Christopher** | Tynemouth | 10b 370 | info ͡ |

Unfortunately Christopher's death indexes were not listed; however, as described shortly, the indexes for his death were subsequently found using Ancestry.co.uk, which is associated with FreeBMD. As mentioned earlier the indexes on FreeBMD are completely free of charge and are part of an ongoing process. I was not able to find Christopher's death because that year had not yet been fully transcribed.

Several more searches were carried out using FreeBMD for other ancestors and these were successful in finding the indexes. The process is obviously much quicker than scanning the sheets by eye. As stated before, there is no charge for searches using FreeBMD.

Referring to the marriage record for Christopher Walls on the previous page, clicking on the link **Tynemouth** opens the GENUKI Web site, giving details about the registration district and links to other villages and parishes in the area.

Clicking on the page number **370** shown on the previous page displays a list of other names on the page including my future (in 1885) grandmother Mary Ann McKeown.

Surname	First name(s)	Age	District	Vol	Page		
	Marriages Sep 1885	(>99%)					
Cresswell	Edward		Tynemouth	10b	370	Info	
McKeown	Mary Ann		Tynemouth	10b	370	Info	
MORPETH	Elizabeth		Tynemouth	10b	370	Info	
Walls	Christopher		Tynemouth	10b	370	Info	

Has our search engine found the record you are seeking?

Click here to learn what to do now.

Found one partner in a marriage but now looking for the spouse?

Click here for more information.

Ordering a Certificate

The important information on the records above and on the previous page are the volume **10b** and the page **370**. These can be used, together with the person's name and the date and place of the birth, marriage or death, to order a certificate from the General Register Office. Make a note of the indexes etc., before starting to order a certificate.

At the bottom left of the screenshot above, there is a link as shown enlarged below. Click the word **here** to continue with the process of ordering a certificate, as described on the next page.

Click here to learn what to do now.

The FreeBMD Web page entitled **Ordering Certificates** opens, including lists of the information to be found on birth, marriage and death certificates. Then you are informed of the two sources of certificates:

- The General Register Office (GRO).
- The local Register Office relevant to the certificate.

Scroll down the FreeBMD **Ordering Certificates** Web page and there is a note on obtaining a certificate as shown below.

Obtaining a certificate from the GRO

For current information on fees and current ordering procedures click here .

You will need the GRO reference, that is the volume and page number given in

---

To order a birth, marriage or death certificate online, click the word **here** shown above. This opens the General Register Office Web page at **www.gro.gov.uk/gro/contents/**.

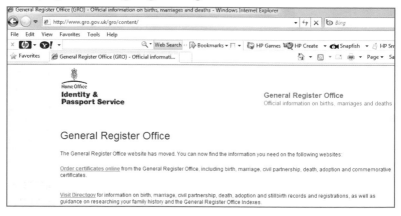

From the General Register Office Web page click the link **Order certificates online** shown above.

This leads to the **Certificate ordering service** page which gives information about what you will need to provide. Click the link **Order a certificate online now**. You are now required to register as a new user, with an e-mail address and a password. You will need the indexes from the search in FreeBMD and the person's name, year and place where the event was registered.

After checking the details, select the sending option for postage and completing the payment procedure. Depending on the sending option chosen, a certified copy of the birth, marriage or death certificate will arrive in the post in a few days time.

Viewing a Scan of an Original Page of Indexes

Marriages Sep 1885 (>99%)

| **Walls** | **Christopher** | | **Tynemouth** | **10b** 370 | **[Info]** 👓 |

The spectacles icon allows you to display a copy of the 👓 original birth, marriage or death indexes in various formats, selected from the list on the right below.

View the original	You can view the original scan that was used to transcribe this entry. The following is the scan file that contains the entry.	Display scan in following format:
	DB-03/1885M3-W-0247.tif	○ gif
		● jpeg
		○ tiff
Help with this facility	Select the format using the buttons on the right and then click on the View the original icon on the left.	○ pdf
Use of this facility is subject to your acceptance of the Terms	If the scan does not contain the entry you may be able to find the scan yourself by clicking here.	○ original
		Which format to choose?

The **original** format is the one used when the page was scanned. The **gif**, **tif** and **jpeg** formats can be viewed on many standard Windows programs. A **pdf file** (portable document format) is opened in the program Adobe Reader, which can be

Display scan in following format:
○ gif
○ jpeg
○ tiff
○ pdf
● original

downloaded free from www.adobe.co.uk. After selecting **View the original**, shown on the left above, you can either **Open** or **Save** the file in your chosen format. Shown below is part of the page of marriage indexes for July, August and September 1885. This has been opened as a **pdf** file in Adobe Reader. You can view a page of indexes, zoom in and out and save a copy of the original document but you can't change or edit the page.

It View Document Tools Window Help
⬛ · ✋   1 / 1   ⊝ ⊕ 150% ·   ⬛ ⬛   Find   ·

247	MARRIAGES registered in July, August, and September 1885.

	District	Vol.	Page			District	Vol.	Page			
WALL, Theobald	Oldham	8d.	973	WALLIS, Kate	Bury	8 c.	678	WALTER, Alice		
——— Thomas	Islington	1 b.	498	——— Lucy	Islington	1 b.	556	——— Amelia Maria		
——— Thomas	Shoreditch	1 c.	269	——— Martha Ann	Nottingham	7 b.	305	——— Andrew Evison		
——— Walter	Keighley	9 a.	257	——— Mary Ann	Poplar	1 c.	983	——— Emily		
——— Walter	Liverpool	8 a.	332	——— Mary Zillah	Daventry	3 b.	210	——— Emily Eliza M.		
——— William	Woolwich	1 d.	1631	——— Richard	Plymouth	5 b.	473	——— Faony Louise		
——— William	Liverpool	8 b.	138	——— Samuel	Nottingham	7 b.	252	——— Frank Thomas		
WALLACE, Adam	Newcastle T.	10 b.	74	——— Sandford	Ashby Z.	7 a.	143	——— Fred		
——— Adélaide Maud M. A.	Bethnal Green	1 c.	353	——— Thomas	Hartlepool	10 a.	140	——— Frederick John		
——— Alexander	Huddersfield	9 a.	556	——— Thomas John	Alton	2 c.	266a	——— Hannah Maria		
——— Ann	Tynemouth	10 b.	369	——— Thomas Walter	Shoreditch	1 c.	214	——— James		
——— Charles	Bramley	9 b.	469	——— William Alfred	Wandsworth	1 d.	956	——— Joseph		
——— Christiana	Ristridge	4 a.	813	——— William Thomas	St. Geo. H. Sq.	1 a.	880	——— Mary Jane		
——— Elizabeth	Chelsea	1 c.	689							

Ancestry.co.uk

This Web site allows you to search all of the census records form 1841 to 1901 and all Civil Registration records of births, marriages and deaths from 1837 to 2005. There are also military and immigration and emigration records.

The birth, marriage and death indexes have been transcribed so that you can now search for a name and an event using the computer, rather than having to go through pages of records on the screen, scanning by eye until you find the entry you want. Ancestry.co.uk uses the FreeBMD transcribed indexes from 1837 to 1915 and its own transcribed indexes from 1916 to 2005.

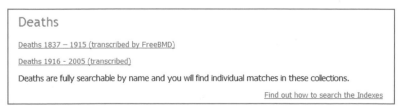

Deaths

Deaths 1837 – 1915 (transcribed by FreeBMD)

Deaths 1916 - 2005 (transcribed)

Deaths are fully searchable by name and you will find individual matches in these collections.

Find out how to search the Indexes

I was trying to obtain the death certificate of my grandfather, Christopher Walls, but this could have occurred in any year between 1911 and about 1940. Scanning the death indexes (four sheets per year) would be a massive task and also expensive, since you have to pay for each page viewed. The transcribed records, searchable by computer, should save all of this effort.

The Ancestry.co.uk Home Page is opened by entering its address into the Address Bar of a browser such as Internet Explorer, as shown below.

From the Home Page you can select either **Search** or **Search All Records**. If you enter a person's name into **Search All Records** you will be given a list of all of the occurrences of their name in all of the registers — births, marriages, deaths, census records and any other record collections. As I was looking for the indexes to order a death certificate I went straight to **the Birth, Marriage & Death** search and then narrowed it down by searching in the **England & Wales Death Index: 1916 — 2005**.

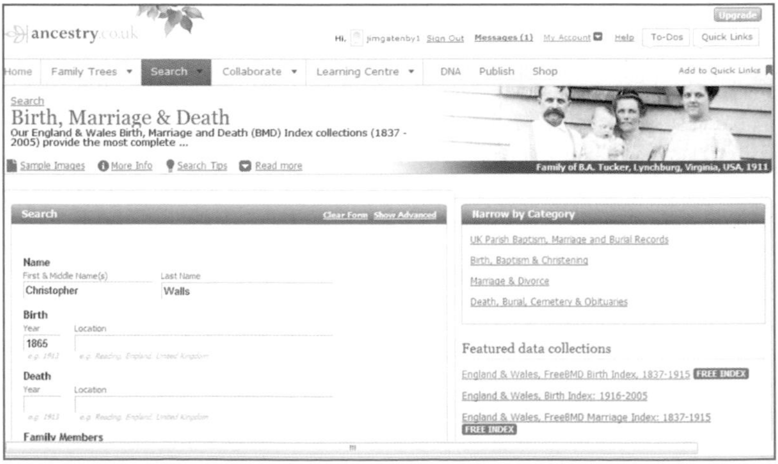

A large number of deaths were found under the name Christopher Walls but the first one shown below looked a good bet. This is because I knew that my mother's family eventually finished up in the North Riding of Yorkshire and also that my father originated from Middlesbrough.

View Record ★★★	Christopher Walls	1937	Middlesbrough	Yorkshire North Riding	🛒	📥
View Record ★★★	Christopher Walls	1947	Wolverhampton	Staffordshire	🛒	📥
View Record ★★★	Christopher Walls	1927	Brentford	Middlesex	🛒	📥
View Record ★★★	Christopher Walls	1936	Wigan	Lancashire	🛒	📥

Clicking on the link **View Record** above displays the fully transcribed record as shown below, with the indexes, etc., needed to order a death certificate.

England & Wales, Death Index: 1916-2005 about Christopher Walls

Name:	**Christopher Walls**
Death Registration Month/Year:	1937
Age at death (estimated):	72
Registration district:	Middlesbrough
Inferred County:	Yorkshire North Riding
Volume:	9d
Page:	569

📥 View original image

Save This Record
Attach this record to a person in your tree as a source record, or save for later evaluation.

Save ▾

There is a link on the previous window to view the original scanned image of the page of deaths. There is also an icon to display the original image on the extreme right of the transcribed record shown below.

| View Record ★★★ | Christopher Walls | 1937 | Middlesbrough | Yorkshire North Riding | 🛒 | 🖼 |

Ordering a Certificate

Click the icon shown on the right and on the record for Christopher Walls above. The **ancestryshop** order form opens as shown below with some of the details already entered. Now, if not entered automatically, enter the year of the birth, marriage or death and the district, volume and page number from the record, as shown on the previous page.

⟩ ancestryshop

| Order Details 🛒 | Delivery Address | Order Summary | Payment |

Death Certificate Order Details
Please be advised that we can only supply Births, Deaths and Marriage certificates from England and Wales. Certificates can be obtained from 1837 to 18 months prior to the present date.

Particulars of the person whose Death Certificate is required   ?

| Surname of Deceased * | Walls |
| Forename(s) of Deceased * | Christopher |

Reference Information from GRO Index   ?

Year (yyyy) *	1937	
Quarter *	3 ▾	OK ✔
District Name *	Middlesbrough	OK ✔
Volume Number *	9d	OK ✔
Page Number *	569	OK ✔

You also need to select the type of postal delivery (standard or express) before clicking **Continue** and completing the order with your personal details and banker's card details.

The Death Certificate

A copy of the death certificate arrived in the post a few days later. Fortunately the deceased Christopher Walls was indeed my grandfather, since everything on the certificate tallied, such as his age in 1937 and his former occupation. The informant was one of my uncles and the area where Christopher Walls had died was one I had visited briefly as a child to meet various relatives.

The information on the above death certificate includes:

- The date and place of death.
- The name, sex and age of the deceased.
- The occupation of the deceased.
- The cause of death.
- The signature, address and description of the informant, who may have been present at the death.

Some death certificates also include the date and place of birth of the deceased and also the name of their spouse, if applicable.

Results of Online Searching

Initially all I knew of my grandfather was his surname, Walls, and the names of some of his children. Using only online searching and BMD certificates ordered online, I found the following:

1865 Birth Record

Christopher Walls, born 9, Church St, Maxwelltown, Dumfries

Father: William (b. Scotland) Mother Elizabeth (b. Ireland).

1871 Census England and Wales

Age 6. Living at Tynemouth, with parents and 5 lodgers.

1881 Census England and Wales

Age 16. Living at Tynemouth with parents. Road labourer.

1885 Marriage Certificate

Married Mary Ann McKeown at Tynemouth. Working as a shipyard labourer.

1888 and 1890 Birth Records

Children Sarah Walls and William Walls born at Lumphinnins, Ballingry, County of Fife, Scotland.

1891 Census England and Wales

Living with wife and children at 12, Town Street, Gateshead, Durham. Working as a general labourer.

1901 Census England and Wales

Living with wife and 5 children at Blue Row, Embleton, Alnwick, Northumberland. Working as whinstone breaker in a quarry.

1911 Census England and Wales

Living with wife and 7 children at Ritton Whitehouse, Ewesley, Rothbury, near Morpeth, Northumberland. Working in a quarry.

1937 Death Certificate

Died at North Ormesby Hospital , Middlesbrough aged 72

All census records above were obtained using findmypast.co.uk. Scottish birth records were extracted using ScotlandsPeople. English birth and marriage certificates were obtained by first obtaining GRO indexes using findmypast.co.uk and then ordering by post from the General Register Office. Christopher Walls' death certificate was ordered after obtaining the GRO indexes using FreeBMD and Ancestry.co.uk. GENUKI, Google, Google Maps and Google Street View were used to find information about places.

Loose Ends

This chapter attempts to investigate a few of the stories and possible connections in our families and ends with a summary of what I believe has been achieved by this online journey.

Exploring the Nautical Connection

My father, Arthur, grew up by the sea in Yorkshire and was involved with boats from an early age. Both he and his brother Ronald spent many years in the merchant navy, my father as an engineer officer and Ronald as a chief engineer. Living in landlocked Derbyshire myself I had never had a close association with the sea; however, while looking through the various birth and marriage certificates in my father's family I discovered that my great grandfather John Hebden was listed as a mariner, shown on the right and below.

One generation farther back than John Hebden, my great, great, grandfather Jonathan is listed at his son John's marriage as a sea captain (deceased).

It was perhaps a sign of those times that when my grandfather Arthur Wright Gatenby and great grandfather John were both married in their twenties, as shown on their marriage certificates on the previous page, both of their fathers were already dead.

Records sent to me by a relative indicated that prior to Jonathan's birth at Egton in 1817 or 1818 many of my relatives were centred around Whitby on the East Coast of Yorkshire.

I used the GENUKI Web site to find out about the history of Whitby, a busy fishing port, particularly whaling. Entering the name of a place like Whitby into GENUKI also reveals a wealth of other information, such as the 13th century ruined abbey and also the fact that Whitby was used for the setting of the film of Count Dracula by Bram Stoker.

Documents 1 - 20 of 1350 matches. More ☆'s indicate a better match.

☆☆☆☆☆ 1. **GENUKI: Whitby Muster Rolls for 1747 (Old Style)**
☆☆☆☆☆ 2. **GENUKI: Whitby Muster Rolls for 1747 (Old Style)**
   ☆☆☆ 3. **GENUKI: Whitby Parish information from Bulmers' 1890.**
   ☆☆☆ 4. **GENUKI: Whitby Parish information from Bulmers' 1890.**
   ☆☆☆ 5. **GENUKI: Whitby History**

However, as I was interested in finding out about my forebears in Whitby I put **Gatenby** and **Whitby** into Google.

The link which appeared at the top of the list of search results is shown below. Clicking on this link displayed the memorial inscription for St. Mary's, Whitby, shown on the next page.

Print Page - Memorial inscription, St. Mary's **Whitby**
27 May 1716 Mary bastard d of Deborah **Gatenby Whitby** ... 26 April 1741 John and Thomas
twin s of Joseph Gatenby sailor of Whitby ...

---

25 May 1712 John s of John Gatenby Whitby
12 April 1713 Hester d of Deborah Gatenby Whitby
27 May 1716 Mary bastard d of Deborah Gatenby Whitby
3 June 1716 Judith d of John Gatenby sailor Whitby
13 July 1718 Richard s of John Gatenby sailor Whitby
17 Dec 1729 William s of Joseph Gatenby Whitby
11 Jan 1735/6 Joseph s of Joseph Gatenby Whitby
6 Jan 1733/4 James s of Joseph Gatenby Whitby
26 April 1741 John and Thomas twin s of Joseph Gatenby sailor of Whitby
24 June 1744 Ann d of Joseph Gatenby Sailor of Whitby
27 June 1741 Thomas s of Joseph Gatenby sailor Whitby
23 Dec 1746 John s of Joseph Gatenby sailor Whitby
5 Nov 1774 Joseph s of Joseph and Mary (tidewaiter) born 3rd Whitby
19 Jan 1806 Joseph Gatenby Pilot 80 years Whitby

John Gatenby at the top of the list above, born Whitby 25 May 1712, appears to be my ancestor John Gatenby, listed on my relative's records but born on the 28th not 25th May 1712, an easy error to make. Most of the men listed above were employed at sea in some capacity; 6 were sailors and one a *pilot* responsible for navigating ships into the harbour. Joseph, the *tidewaiter* was apparently a customs officer who boarded ships to enforce the law. The status of Mary shown above would no doubt be described in a more sympathetic way in the 21st Century.

By entering searches such as **J Gatenby Mariner** into Google I was able to find that a J Gatenby sailed with Captain Cook (himself raised near Whitby) on his ship the Discovery. Also that a Captain J Gatenby was the master on the ship Nimroud of Scarborough taking emigrants to a new life in Australia in1855.

Mariners and ships in Australian Waters
NIMROUD

SHIP OF SCARBORO, J. GATENBY MASTER, BURTHEN 1022 TONS
FROM THE PORT OF LONDON TO SYDNEY NEW SOUTH WALES, 18TH OCTOBER 1855

Surname	Given name	Station	Age	Of what Nation	Status	Comments
GATENBY	J.	CAPTAIN			CREW	
FRASER	T.	MATE	26	G. B.	CREW	
HERALD	WM. JAMES	2ND MATE	32	G. B.	CREW	
POWNEY	R. C.	SURGEON	29	G. B.	CREW	

Emigration

I could not be certain that the J Gatenby who sailed with Captain Cook on the Discovery or the Captain of the ship Nimroud taking immigrants to Australia were my close relatives. However, I had found enough evidence to be sure that many of my ancestors were involved with the sea.

Many people left England for a new life in Australia, New Zealand and Canada. Some of these immigrants prospered, such as my father's brother Harold Heslop Gatenby, who went to Canada in 1927 aged 22. Using the **Migration / Passenger Lists Leaving UK 1890-1960** feature in findmypast.co.uk I was able to find the original record for Harold's voyage, as shown below.

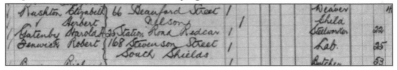

The fully transcribed record of Harold's voyage is shown below. His wife, Maude Mary, aged 20 years followed in September of the same year in the Albertic bound for Montreal.

passenger transcript details		
Name:	**Harold H GATENBY**	PRINTER FRIENDLY VERSION
Date of departure:	**1 June 1927**	
Port of departure:	**Liverpool**	
Passenger destination port:	**Quebec, Canada**	VIEW ORIGINAL IMAGE
Passenger destination:	**Quebec, Canada**	
Date of Birth:	**1905 (calculated from age)**	
Age:	**22**	
Marital status:		
Sex:	**Male**	
Occupation:	**Steelworker**	
Passenger recorded on:	**Page 1 of 12**	
Ship:	**CALGARIC**	
Official Number:	**140579**	
Master's name:	**J Kearney**	
Steamship Line:	**White Star**	REPORT TRANSCRIPTION CHANGE
Where bound:	**Montreal, Canada**	
Square feet:	**10701**	
Registered tonnage:	**16063**	
Passengers on voyage:	**234**	

As shown in Mark Gatenby's family tree on page 2, Harold and Maude went on to produce a substantial Canadian family of their own and, as far as I know, never returned to England.

Grandma in the Workhouse?

I had found plenty of evidence about my maternal grandmother from her marriage certificate dated 1885 and in the subsequent censuses up to 1911. However, I was unable to find any record of her in the censuses for 1871 and 1881, when she should have been living in the Newcastle area, where she was born in 1867. However, there was a girl of the right age listed in the Tynemouth Union Workhouse in the 1881 Census; the only problem was that her name was given as Mary McKune, not Mary McKeown, as given on the marriage certificate and on the various censuses.

However, it does seem quite likely that this was my grandmother since four years after this 1881 Census, my grandmother was married at Tynemouth, according to the marriage certificate. By this time she was aged 18 years, the same age as the girl in the Tynemouth Union Workhouse would have been.

According to the marriage certificate, my grandmother's father was already dead at her marriage in 1885 and this could explain why she and her sister had been "inmates" (as they were called) of the Tynemouth Union Workhouse. Also, getting married at the age of 18 might have been a way to escape the workhouse. The difference in spelling of the name is not too surprising in those times of limited educational opportunity — my grandfather had to use a cross for his "signature" on their marriage certificate.

Famous Names

Most of us would probably like to think we were connected to someone famous, successful or perhaps even notorious. In Jill's family there is a widely held view that they are related to Dr. Samuel Johnson, creator of the first dictionary and the subject of James Boswell's biography "Life of Samuel Johnson".

Samuel Johnson

Doctor Johnson's father Michael (born 1658) and his grandfather William lived in a very small hamlet called Great Cubley in Derbyshire. Jill's ancestors, also called Johnson, lived at the same time a stone's throw away in the neighbouring hamlet of Mockley, between the parishes of Cubley and Sudbury. It was a very sparsely populated rural area, so the chances of Jill's ancestors being related to Samuel Johnson's family seem quite strong. Typing **Samuel Johnson** into Google produces a wealth of information about the great man.

Unfortunately the main genealogy Web sites do not generally go back this far in time. However, from the GENUKI Web site I found out that the church records (known as Bishops' Transcripts) for Cubley and Sudbury are kept at the Lichfield Joint Record Office. We hope to visit this office in the near future and explore the Dr. Johnson connection further.

Andrew Gatenby

On my father's side, Andrew Gatenby was a struggling farmer from the Whitby area of Yorkshire who emigrated to Van Diemen's Land (Tasmania) via a farm in the Brecon Beacons. He later became a successful landowner with several estates, apart from being a chief police constable, well-known cattle breeder and church benefactor. With his sons he founded the Penny Royal Corn Mill, which has since become a visitor attraction and holiday complex. Andrew's achievements can be found on numerous Web sites by entering **Andrew Gatenby Tasmania** into a search engine such as Google.

Penny Royal World

Thursday, July 31, 2003

Catriona shows us a very fun side of Tassie; and this favourite fun park is going off.

A visit to Penny Royal World is like stepping back into the 19th century. Its story is of Andrew Gatenby, an early pioneer of van Dieman's land, and his family. They arrived in 1823 and settled on land between Cressy and Ross on the Isis River, then known as Penny Royal Creek. They built their farmhouse and millhouse there.

Penny Royal World

Andrew Gatenby was born in 1771 in the small village of Egton, and his wife Hannah (née Maw) was born at nearby Whitby. My great, great grandfather Jonathan Gatenby was born at Egton in 1818. It has been suggested that Andrew Gatenby was probably the uncle of Jonathan. Andrew died in Tasmania in 1848, aged 77, while Hannah reached 100 years of age. Their gravestones are shown below in the family's private cemetery on their own land in Tasmania, a far cry from their roots in the North Riding of Yorkshire and their farm in the Brecon Beacons in Wales.

This photo was taken by my cousin John Lansdale Gatenby during a visit to relatives in Tasmania. It was then sent straight to my computer as an e-mail attachment in the form of a jpg file. (Also known as a JPEG file, a common photographic format).

What Can You Learn from Online Research?

I knew nothing of my grandfather, Christopher Walls, before starting this research. He died before I was born, my parents didn't talk of him and we lived in a different part of the country from the rest of the family. Online computer research enabled me to discover the major events in Christopher's life — where he was born, the many places where he lived with his family, where he worked and the date, place and cause of his death.

I discovered that Christopher was born in Scotland, of Scottish and Irish parents and that both his wife's parents were Irish. Having thought of myself as totally English, I found that of my eight great grandparents, three were Irish and one Scottish. Many of us probably have surprisingly mixed backgrounds; knowing this might lead to different attitudes to other people.

I also found out that many of my ancestors were employed in simple, traditional jobs at sea, in farming or labouring in shipyards and quarries. Less than 100 years ago, my grandfather Christopher Walls, unable to write his own name, worked in quarries around Northumberland; Jill's grandfather, James Brunt, farmed in the Staffordshire Moorlands, near the (allegedly) lawless village of Flash. How different from the 21st century jobs of two of their great grandsons; one (also called James Brunt) is now the sales director in Japan for a prestigious multi-national car company and the Honorary British Consul for Okinawa; the other is an airline pilot flying Boeing 707s between Europe and the Middle East.

As someone who spent many years as both a pupil and teacher in inner city schools it was interesting to discover my own rural roots. Having married into a farming family I no longer felt such an outsider. Most of us should be able to find some country cousins if we go back far enough. Realising this should reduce the tensions which sometimes exist between town and country dwellers. Tracing you family history online is not expensive and may change you life – it's never too late!

Index